Bon Appétit®
Winter
COOKBOOK

Bon Appétit®

Winter
COOKBOOK

Arabella Boxer and Tessa Traeger

The Knapp Press, Publishers, Los Angeles

Bon Appétit ® is a registered trademark of Bon Appétit
Publishing Corp used with permission

Editor	*Fiona Grafton*
Art Editor	*Val Hobson*
Assistant Editor	*Jane Garton*
Consultant Editor	*Helen Scott-Harman*
Editorial Assistants	*Atalanta Grant-Suttie*
	Amanda Lynch
Assistant Art Editor	*Ingrid Mason*
Art Assistant	*Flick Ekins*
Executive Editor	*Alexandra Towle*

Food and Wine Consulting Editor for The Knapp Press,
Gene Benton, in association with the Editors of Bon Appétit

Bon Appétit Summer and Winter Cookbook was edited and
designed by Mitchell Beazley Publishers Limited, Mill House,
87-89 Shaftesbury Avenue, London W1V 7AD

© Mitchell Beazley Publishers Limited 1980
Text © Arabella Boxer   Photographs © Tessa Traeger and
Condé Nast Publications Limited

First published in the USA by The Knapp Press
5900 Wilshire Boulevard, Los Angeles, California 90036

Distributed by The Viking Press, 625 Madison Avenue, New York,
New York, 10022   Distributed simultaneously in Canada by
Penguin Books Canada Limited

Library of Congress Cataloging in Publication Data

Boxer, Arabella, Lady.
Bon appétit winter cookbook.

Issued with the author's Bon appétit summer cookbook.
Los Angeles (1980)   Inverted text.
Includes indexes.
1. Cookery. I. Traeger, Tessa. II. Title.
III. Title: Winter cookbook.
TX651.B64   641.5'91   79-21133
ISBN 0-89535-036-X

Printed and bound in Great Britain

The publishers and authors would like to thank Jan Baldwin,
Tessa Traeger's assistant, and Oula Jones who compiled the indexes.

Contents

How to use this book . . . . .
The Summer and Winter Cookbook is presented as two books
bound together under one cover. Each book is divided into two sections.
The illustrated text on seasonal cookery themes is cross-referenced to the recipe section.
The index for the Winter Cookbook begins on page 127.

Introduction

During the winter months we become more than ever dependent on our food, particularly in the British Isles. It helps us to keep warm and is of course essential to provide the energy to do any sort of work, whether mental or physical. During the enervating winter months, even vegetable lovers like myself feel the need of more protein, usually in the form of meat. Stews and roasts, that might seem too heavy at other times of the year, are especially welcome in cold weather, as are the filling winter soups made with combinations of fresh and dried vegetables, grains and pastas.

In contrast to these substantial dishes, we have shellfish, rich in iodine and mineral salts, at their best during the cooler months. Moules marinières, clam chowder, broiled Dublin Bay prawns, seviche of scallops, oyster stew, stuffed mussels and clams in aspic are all appetizing and nutritious dishes that can either be served as first courses or as less filling alternatives to meat dishes.

Smoked fish is also excellent during the winter, since autumn is the customary time for smoking. Scottish kippers and smoked mackerel, haddock and cod are all available to us for making into delicious smooth pâtés, or for serving in conjunction with poached or scrambled eggs. The more expensive smoked salmon, sturgeon, halibut and eel are also in the shops; these are best eaten simply with lemons and brown bread and butter.

Roasts of beef and tender broiled steaks are among our favorite winter dishes for festive occasions, while stews, casseroles and meat pies are popular for sustaining, everyday meals. Lamb provides a wide range of good dishes, like roast leg of lamb, braised shoulder of lamb and broiled lamb chops as well as stews like Lancashire hot pot, Irish stew and the French *navarin d'agneau*. Roast pork is a popular Sunday luncheon dish in England, served with applesauce.

We have our black Bradenham hams and Alderton gammons which rival for flavor the delicious sweet-cured hams of the southern United States. (Gammon is the equivalent to a ham but is not separated from the entire side of the pig before the curing process, as are hams.)

Game makes a welcome appearance during the winter months. Grouse and pheasant remain two of the favorite luxuries in Britain and quail, now farmed domestically, are obtainable all year round. Sadly, there is no British equivalent to the delicious American squab; our wild pigeons are much coarser and tougher, and there is no breeding of them especially for the table. Venison is much loved by some, as is hare.

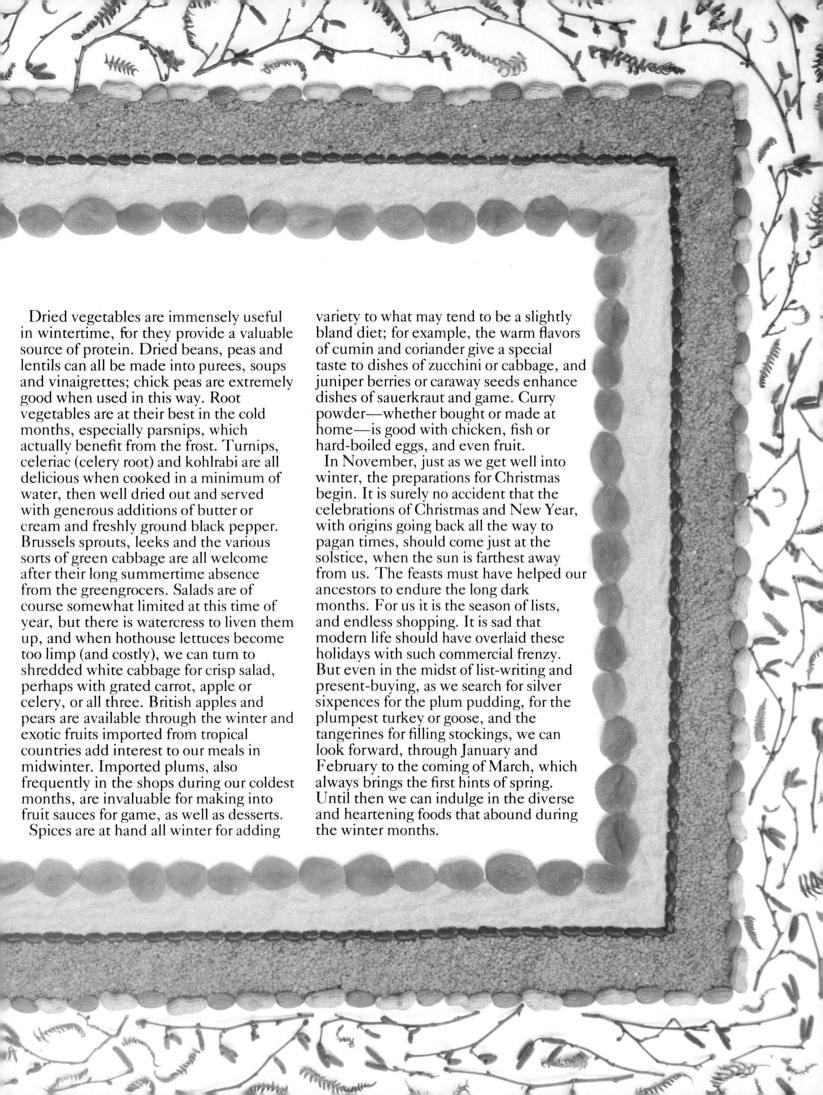

Dried vegetables are immensely useful in wintertime, for they provide a valuable source of protein. Dried beans, peas and lentils can all be made into purees, soups and vinaigrettes; chick peas are extremely good when used in this way. Root vegetables are at their best in the cold months, especially parsnips, which actually benefit from the frost. Turnips, celeriac (celery root) and kohlrabi are all delicious when cooked in a minimum of water, then well dried out and served with generous additions of butter or cream and freshly ground black pepper. Brussels sprouts, leeks and the various sorts of green cabbage are all welcome after their long summertime absence from the greengrocers. Salads are of course somewhat limited at this time of year, but there is watercress to liven them up, and when hothouse lettuces become too limp (and costly), we can turn to shredded white cabbage for crisp salad, perhaps with grated carrot, apple or celery, or all three. British apples and pears are available through the winter and exotic fruits imported from tropical countries add interest to our meals in midwinter. Imported plums, also frequently in the shops during our coldest months, are invaluable for making into fruit sauces for game, as well as desserts.

Spices are at hand all winter for adding variety to what may tend to be a slightly bland diet; for example, the warm flavors of cumin and coriander give a special taste to dishes of zucchini or cabbage, and juniper berries or caraway seeds enhance dishes of sauerkraut and game. Curry powder—whether bought or made at home—is good with chicken, fish or hard-boiled eggs, and even fruit.

In November, just as we get well into winter, the preparations for Christmas begin. It is surely no accident that the celebrations of Christmas and New Year, with origins going back all the way to pagan times, should come just at the solstice, when the sun is farthest away from us. The feasts must have helped our ancestors to endure the long dark months. For us it is the season of lists, and endless shopping. It is sad that modern life should have overlaid these holidays with such commercial frenzy. But even in the midst of list-writing and present-buying, as we search for silver sixpences for the plum pudding, for the plumpest turkey or goose, and the tangerines for filling stockings, we can look forward, through January and February to the coming of March, which always brings the first hints of spring. Until then we can indulge in the diverse and heartening foods that abound during the winter months.

*A*utumn soups

Lighter than the meat-based soups of deep winter, autumn soups combine the last of summer's fresh vegetables with the comforting nourishment of dried peas and beans

For those of us who rely on fresh produce, a whole range of new dishes comes into season in early autumn, some of which cannot be made at any other time of the year. These are vegetable soups that combine the last of the summer's fresh vegetables with the first crop of dried vegetables, at their best at this time. My recipes are from Italy, France and Spain for the most part. They are full of flavor, yet less heavy than the meat-based soups of the true winter months. One of the best is a bean soup from Tuscany, made with the new season's *cannellini* beans, fresh juicy garlic, and the first of the virgin oil, that aromatic green substance which results from the first pressing of the olives. Another is *ribollita*; the name means literally "re-boiled," for it is traditionally made with the remains of yesterday's minestrone, reheated and poured over an unusual purple cabbage called *cavolo nero*, which comes into season in October in Tuscany and the surrounding region. Almost best of all is the Genoese *zuppa al pesto*, a thick soup made with a mixture of fresh and dried beans, and imbued with a fragrant mixture of pounded basil, pine nuts and Parmesan cheese. The Italians also make an excellent pumpkin soup in the autumn, for the pumpkin is at its best when combined with the sweet taste of fresh basil, a tender annual which perishes with the first frost. Another good soup which is not often seen outside its native Italy is *pasta e fagioli*, a combination of dried haricot beans with spaghetti, cooked with bacon and fresh vegetables, and flavored with garlic.

An unusual soup is made from dried chick peas; this is popular in Spain, in Italy and parts of Mediterranean France. Another and most delicious soup which is found all over Spain in varying forms is the *sopa del ajo*, or garlic soup. As served to me in a restaurant in Granada, it consisted of a thin garlic-flavored broth poured over a poached egg and pieces of bread in a capacious bowl. Many of these continental soups have bread in them, and ideally it should be homemade. If this is not possible, try to buy an unsliced crusty white loaf of coarse texture, and keep it for a day or two before using.

Many Italian soups also have an egg in them, and these make light sustaining meals, easily digested even when one is tired. One of the best is *zuppa pavese*, where a whole egg is either lightly poached in chicken stock, or simply placed raw in a warm bowl, and very lightly coddled in the heat of the chicken broth which is poured over it. Another, *stracciatella*, consists of chicken stock with a couple of raw eggs beaten and stirred into the soup while boiling. It is allowed to boil gently for a moment or two, being stirred constantly, so that the egg is cooked in shreds. A similar soup is the Greek *avgolemono*; here the eggs are beaten with lemon juice and stirred into the soup below boiling point. The clear chicken broth is thus enriched and slightly thickened by the eggs, and flavored with the lemon, to make a smooth and delicious soup.

With the exception of *zuppa al pesto*, which needs fresh beans and basil, most of these soups can be made throughout the winter, but are at their freshest and best in October and early November. Even the heavy French dishes like *potée* and *garbures* take on a lighter character when made with fresh, albeit elderly, peas and beans. The soups containing dried beans are very filling, and can be treated as a meal in themselves, possibly with a fresh salad and cheese. They take a long time to make, and I now use a pressure cooker, which works out well. The base of mine is a bit thin for prolonged frying, so I sometimes use a heavy sauté pan for the first stage, then transfer the contents to the pressure cooker for the lengthy simmering, which is thus cut by two-thirds. On the other hand, the lighter soups, those with eggs and chicken stock, are made in a matter of minutes, always providing you have a supply of good chicken stock already made. These delicate soups are just not worth making with stock cubes. If I am alone, I often make a light meal of one of these, usually *zuppa pavese*, which is easily made for one. They can also serve as the first course for a conventional meal.

All these soups are improved by some last-minute addition. The bean soup and the *ribollita* should have a little fresh olive oil (ideally green Tuscan oil) added just before eating. Chopped parsley can be substituted by those who are not enamored of olive oil. Freshly grated Parmesan cheese is an important part of the Italian soups made with eggs and chicken stock, but I have used Fontina, Pecorino, and even Gruyère or Emmenthal on occasions. All vegetable soups are improved by salt and coarsely ground black pepper, added by each individual to his taste.

1 Tuscan bean soup
2 Vicchio Maggio, a classic Chianti
3 Italian bread
4 Garlic
5 Cannellini beans
6 Parsley

Favorite first courses

Delectable, pretty and colorful hors d'oeuvre can either make a complete meal in themselves or give distinction to a meal by setting the tone for what is to follow

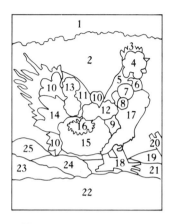

1 Shredded iceberg lettuce
2 Sliced cucumber
3 Carrot
4 Snails, zucchini, lemon
5 Salami
6 Onions
7 Goat cheese in chestnut leaves
8 Camembert cheese
9 Pepper goat cheese
10 Mussels
11 Dover sole
12 Baked oysters with sorrel and
  green peppercorn sauce
13 Baked oysters with shredded
  vegetables
14 Red mullet
15 Crab
16 Parsley
17 Lobster
18 Runner beans, lemon and orange
  peel
19 Runner beans
20 Fennel
21 Fish pâté
22 Prosciutto ham, peas, beans,
  carrots, potato
23 Mange-tout peas
24 Mixed shredded vegetables
25 Sliced zucchini

From a psychological point of view, the first course of a meal is the most important. If it is pretty and interesting and tastes marvelous, it will elevate the tone of the whole meal, and the rest can be kept relatively simple. If, on the other hand, it is dull or depressing, nothing that follows will redeem the meal. I take more trouble over the first course for a dinner than over any other, partly for the reasons given above, and partly because it is my favorite course.

Almost all the dishes I like best qualify as first courses; in restaurants I often find it hard to choose from so many appealing things, while the list of main courses may not tempt me at all. Little dishes made from combinations of pastry, pasta, pancakes or rice with vegetables, eggs or shellfish seem to me more attractive than the serious heavy dishes which in restaurant terms qualify as main courses. There is of course no reason why those of us who feel this way should not treat ourselves to a series of first-course dishes, either together or in sequence, to form a complete meal at home.

My favorite first courses are pretty and colorful, so that they provide a table decoration in themselves: little pastry cases filled with sliced mushrooms in a cream sauce; a gratin of hard-boiled eggs and onions in a creamy sauce; green pancakes rolled around fillings of chopped tomato in sour cream; a mixture of smoked and fresh haddock, flaked in a creamy cheese sauce; curried eggs; green gnocchi; stuffed tomatoes; and little skewers of firm white fish, basted with olive oil and lemon juice while broiling.

Many of these dishes are quite a lot of trouble to prepare, although almost all are greatly accelerated by the food processor, as they are based on pastry, batter, or purees of raw fish or meat. A few of them, like green gnocchi, skewers of fish, and pancakes, must be made at the last moment; others, like the mushrooms in pastry cases, can be prepared in advance and assembled just before serving. The gratins of egg and of haddock can be made beforehand, and only reheated and browned before serving. Pâtés can, of course, be made days in advance.

I like to serve very small portions of two or three different hot dishes as a first course, as in a small restaurant in Rome which I remember. There each evening they served three different hot hors d'oeuvre. One could eat them separately if one wished, but they were planned to complement each other; for example a slice of onion quiche served with a spoonful of vegetables stewed with oil, and a slice of hot fish pâté.

When I am serving a homemade pâté, I have with it warm, freshly baked bread and a dish of mixed vegetables, perhaps sliced fennel and tomatoes, stewed in oil and served warm. Sometimes I make three different hot, or warm, vegetable dishes: string beans with chopped bacon, sliced mushrooms in sour cream, and grilled tomatoes with garlic and parsley butter melting over them. These dishes are greatly enhanced by the homemade bread, possibly a slightly unusual one like onion bread or saffron bread. After a series of dishes like this, only the simplest main course need follow, such as beef stew, a roast chicken, or a whole fish, baked or poached, served with a complementary sauce.

$\mathcal{S}$ustaining soups

Warming and restoring, a stout winter soup is a meal in its own right. With the right accompaniments, a good soup will rise to almost any occasion

If I had to choose one type of food to live on for the rest of my life, I would probably settle for soup. I can think of no other dish which covers such a wide range, and I am sure I could think up a different one for every day in the year if I put my mind to it; I have made a list of over seventy without even trying very hard.

I like almost all sorts of soup: thick hearty potages; creamy vegetable purees; clear consommés, either hot or jellied; chowders made from fish and vegetables; and iced summer soups. In winter, though, I concentrate on the nourishing peasant type—not an elegant start for a meal to be drunk out of small cups, but a meal in itself to be consumed from large bowls and needing little to follow, perhaps a raw vegetable salad or a platter of cheeses with celery. These soups are warming and restoring. They are nourishing but not too time-consuming or expensive to make. They improve with reheating, so they can be prepared in advance and in large quantities, and thus they can feed an unexpected number of people, should such an occasion arise.

All too often soup is considered a way of using up remains rather than as a dish in its own right; or it is added to a meal as an afterthought, to give a warming element, or to stretch the amount of food offered. I, on the other hand, tend to think of the soup first and plan a meal around it, or even a succession of meals. On the weekend I often buy a large chicken and poach it; I then make a chicken and barley soup from the stock, and on the following day I make a dish from the bird itself: a chicken pie, noodle dish or a chicken salad. The carcass is then used to make a second supply of slightly weaker stock, which makes another soup, perhaps a vichyssoise or an *avgolemono*. During the winter I often buy a grouse and make a game pâté from the flesh of the bird and an excellent lentil soup from the stock. A splendid borsch can be made for a family dinner by using a duck for making the stock;

pirozhkis can be served with it to form an almost complete meal, and then the duck itself eaten cold the following day, perhaps with a hot dish of rice, pine nuts and raisins, and a salad of watercress and oranges.

I have experimented with the idea of adding a piquant taste to the soup at the last moment, as one adds the *pistou* to a soup of the same name, or *rouille* to a bouillabaisse. I find that a minestrone is enormously improved by the last-minute addition of a paste similar to a *pistou* but made with winter alternatives. A few spoonfuls of onions and garlic gently fried in olive oil can with advantage be added to a soup made from dried vegetables—peas, lentils or beans. It is common practice in parts of France to add something of this sort—called *la fricassée* or *le hachis*—to soups; sometimes a spoonful of the vegetables from the soup chopped and fried in goose or bacon fat, or a mix of bacon, onion and garlic cooked in oil.

The method is similar to one I have come across in Middle Eastern recipes and in some Indian dishes, in which a measure of freshly cooked onions is added to a dish that has been cooked for a long time, thus adding texture and freshness. In some curries, the chopped onions are divided in two parts, the one forming the basis of the curry and the other fried in clarified butter and added at the very end, by which time the first lot have cooked away to an indistinguishable puree.

It is only when made with care and thought that soups are as good as they should be, but when they are, they are very rewarding. They respond well to accompaniments such as carefully chosen bread—a saffron bread with a fish soup, garlic bread with minestrone, black rye bread for cabbage soup. A bowl of salt, a peppermill filled with black peppercorns, and some unsalted butter should always be on the table; and a bowl of chopped parsley or freshly grated Parmesan cheese is indicated in many cases. And in general, hearty winter soups are enhanced by the use of a fine tureen and pretty soup bowls.

1 Portuguese cabbage soup
2 Green cabbage
3 Red kidney beans
4 Kabanos (Polish sausage)
5 Parsley
6 Rice
7 Watercress
8 Salt
9 Sausage and vegetable ingredients
   for the soup

Smoked fish

An ancient method of preserving made unnecessary by technology, the smoking of fish continues to create myriad subtle flavors for the discriminating palate

1 *Kippered herring*
2 *Smoked mackerel*
3 *Smoked eel*
4 *Smoked cod's roe*
5 *Smoked trout*
6 *Smoked mackerel fillet*
7 *Smoked sprats*

baked smoked fish p75
smoked salmon pâté p79
smoked mackerel pâté p80
smokie pâté p80
kipper pâté p80

Smoked fish have for many years been among Great Britain's most famous delicacies. No other country can improve upon Scotch smoked salmon or Loch Fyne kippers. Smoked eel is delicious, but unfortunately almost as expensive as smoked salmon. Another expensive one is smoked sturgeon—not, in my opinion, worth the high price it commands.

One fish which I like very much smoked is halibut, and perhaps my favorite of all is the "Arbroath smokie"; this is a small haddock smoked whole, quite unlike the more familiar smoked haddock which has yellow flesh and needs to be cooked. I find smoked mackerel a bit oily to eat plain, but it is among the best-flavored of fish for making into pâtés and mousses.

Smoking was originally a method of preserving food, usually pork or fish, during the winter months. Over the past thirty years, however, the process has changed radically. For one thing, the traditional smokehouse operation was a home-based one, which did not lend itself to expansion, and additionally, the problem of finding suitable fuel became acute. The smokehouses grew up alongside shipyards or carpentry shops, which kept them supplied with oak sawdust, the ideal fuel for smoking food. With mechanization the sawdusts became mixed and hardly suitable. Then it was discovered that the three effects which smoke imposed upon food could be achieved more simply by other means: the preservation was more easily effected by refrigeration, the coloring by dyes, and the flavoring by brief periods of curing and smoking or in some cases by merely painting the food with liquid "smoke flavor," a concentrate of distilled smoke. The result was inevitably a different product, for it was a smoke-flavored food rather than a smoke-cured one.

Defenders of the modern methods claim that the stronger flavors of traditionally smoked fish would not appeal to the modern palate, which has become accustomed to blander things. This is probably true, and certainly is in extreme cases like the red herring, which was so strongly cured and smoked that it could be kept without refrigeration from one season to the next.

I once spent a fascinating day with a man who has made a prolonged study of the smoking of food, and has worked out his own way of producing traditional results. Mr. Pinney is in his late sixties and has lived near Woodbridge in Suffolk for the past thirty years. He gradually built up a smoking business and other enterprises over the years. Now, with the help of his wife Mathilde and his son Billy he runs an oyster hatchery, two fishing boats and a smokehouse. He is an extremely interesting person with enormous enterprise and imagination. Some twenty years ago, faced with the difficulty of finding an adequate supply of oak sawdust, he took the nearest possible alternative in the form of oak logs, and set about inventing a stove which would burn them in such a way as to produce smoke without much heat. On holiday once in Portugal, finding himself with nothing to do, he built a portable smokebox for smoking the local seafood, which he then sold to the nearest hotel.

Smoking by traditional methods is a fairly primitive process, except for the smoke production which must be very precise. When wood is heated, a succession of different vapors is released, each at a different temperature. The most suitable are those released at a low heat, as they get progressively more acid. While the first smoke is sweet and hazy blue in color, the smoke which is produced at higher temperatures is acrid, rank and yellowish grey.

The main virtue of sawdust as a fuel is that it will not burn naturally at a high temperature because the minute particles restrict the oxygen intake. Most modern smoking equipment subjects the sawdust to a forced draught, thus raising the temperature. In some cases moisture is added, introducing steam, which formerly had no place in the smoking process. Mr. Pinney, doubtful about both these refinements, proceeded to develop his own stove, which by a degree of oxygen control allows him to retain carbon dioxide around the unburned logs, causing them to smoke without allowing them to burn. In this way the wood is converted into charcoal, which he then uses for the second process; there are two stages in smoking fish: cold-smoking and hot-smoking. Both these terms are misnomers, for there is some heat in cold-smoking, while hot-smoking is virtually a cooking process involving no smoke at all. Most fish undergo both processes, except salmon and kippers which are cold-smoked only (kippers are, of course, almost invariably cooked before eating). Mr. Pinney smokes Irish salmon, herrings, sprats, mackerel, trout, eels, pollan (a member of the salmon family) and cod's roe. All this is done in a smokehouse no larger than two sentry boxes back to back.

Shellfish – naturally

Though they are exclusive and highly prized, lobsters, mussels, scallops, clams, crabs and shrimps are among our most natural and primitive forms of food

I find I become more and more attached to the few foods that still retain their own individual character, and cannot be tampered with. Shellfish are among the most primitive of foods; not only do they taste and smell of the sea, even their appearance is redolent of natural things. There is a curious feeling about handling food that is still actually living; while we were photographing what appeared to be a *nature morte*, the mussels suddenly started making the strangest kissing noises—opening and closing in protest, I imagine, at the heat of the lamps. Although I am very squeamish about having to actually kill something in order to cook it, at the same time I cannot help appreciating the inevitable freshness that is the result. Shellfish are certainly the least plastic of foods, and in an age when more and more foods are losing their individual flavor, this is a valuable characteristic.

It was only recently that I started cooking shellfish again. Apart from seaside holidays, I had grown lazy and had managed to convince myself that they were either too expensive—like lobster —or too much trouble to prepare—like mussels and crab. Now I have overcome this resistance and am totally won over. Lobsters are certainly expensive all over the world; even on remote Greek islands they now fetch a startling price. But there are other shellfish just as delicious. Mussels, for instance, are one of the cheapest foods, especially in relation to their goodness and the valuable amounts of iron and calcium they contain. They are a certain amount of trouble to clean, and I would not think of preparing *moules marinières* for more than four people, but there are other ways of treating them, using smaller quantities. They make a good risotto, or a rice salad, or they can be made into an unusual first course by steaming them open, dipping the mussels in egg and bread crumbs, and deep frying. Or they can be threaded on skewers and grilled. Mussels make a delicious soup, and are good stuffed: cover each mussel on a half-shell with a mound of bread crumbs, finely minced shallot, garlic and parsley, dot with butter and brown in the broiler.

Scallops are another beautiful food, and full of flavor. Their shells make pretty dishes for serving them. I usually poach scallops in a mixture of white wine and water, then chop them into pieces and mix with minced shallots in a sauce made from the cooking liquid blended with cream. They are then piled back into their concave shells, sprinkled with parsley and bread crumbs and browned in the broiler. Other ways to serve them are in a mild curry-flavored sauce, or as part of a mixed fish salad. They also make an excellent *seviche*, marinated in fresh lime or lemon juice, and dressed with oil and herbs. Frozen scallops are quite good but expensive. Keep a few shells for serving the frozen ones in, when fresh ones are unobtainable.

Clams are for me an important part of memories of childhood holidays in Maine. In London I buy large clams, not unlike the New England quahog; though full of flavor they are quite tough and not suitable for steaming. They are quite adequate for chowders, and dishes using minced clams. They are not expensive, as two or three per person will be ample.

Dressing a crab at home is time-consuming work, so I think the answer is to buy it already dressed and add the final touches oneself. I do not care much for the brown meat, so I only use a little of this, or omit it altogether. I add other things, like chopped hard-boiled eggs, capers and herbs; then I moisten it with oil and lemon juice and pile it back in the shell. Alternatively, finely chopped avocado can be mixed with the flaked white meat, then flavored with plenty of lemon juice and black pepper.

Prawns, shrimps and crayfish come in varying sizes, ranging down to a miniscule shrimp. The larger prawns are very handsome, and should be served simply in their shells, with a bowl of homemade mayonnaise. Smaller ones can be made into a fresh-tasting summery pâté, tart, with plenty of lemon juice; or rolled in thin slices of bacon threaded on skewers and broiled. They can be served as a first course, with remoulade sauce or quarters of lemon, or on a bed of rice as a main course. Finally, they can be mixed with other shellfish in a salad or rice dish; but when really fresh, I think they are best eaten simply with lemon quarters and thinly sliced brown bread and butter.

1 *Saffron rice and shellfish*
2 *Lobster; clam; mussels; Dublin Bay prawns*
3 *Oysters*
4 *Dressed crab*
5 *Stuffed clam*
6 *Moules gratinées*
7 *Skewered prawns in bacon*
8 *Shrimp pâté*
9 *Coquilles St. Jacques*
10 *Avocado relish*
11 *Tomato vinaigrette sauce*

The best of beef

Festive roasts and noble sirloins, tender steaks and hearty stews, with all the traditional accompaniments, will sustain you through the long, dark months

1 Roast ribs of beef
2 Beef stew
3 Boiled beef
4 Steak tartare
5 Beef olives
6 Horseradish sauce
7 Boiled beef with dumplings
8 Sirloin steak

"Beef is the soul of cookery," Carême once said, and I am totally in agreement. The bull is a noble animal, and the fact that roast beef has been a symbol of England for centuries is a source of pride. English beef cookery, with a strength and character of its own, owes nothing to foreign influence. A standing rib roast, like the one in the picture (which we call a "wing" roast because of its shape), or a thick and juicy grilled steak—these are among the few gastronomic delights that do not seem to have deteriorated in recent years. Even without the traditional English accompaniments—Yorkshire pudding, hot mustard and horseradish sauce—with only the clear, unthickened pan juices, such beef cannot be improved upon. When I lived in Scotland as a child, our Sunday "joint" was invariably a roast sirloin, for it was my father's favorite food.

In those days, the sirloin always came in "porterhouse" form with the fillet, intact, nestling against the bone, basted with its marrow and protected by the flap of rib ends folded over it, and deliciously moist. Nowadays, there is such an insatiable demand for the whole fillet (tenderloin) or its steaks that most British butchers are now handling these cuts more as Americans do. To me a whole roast fillet always seems rather an effete thing; it is too soft somehow, and lacking in character. Possibly because it is often treated in a rather decadent way, smeared with *pâté de foie* and wrapped in pastry, it has come to symbolize the food of the ultra-rich. Even fillet steaks do not appeal to me; I prefer a sirloin steak or the boneless, between-ribs French *entrecôte*, to me far more desirable in flavor, texture and appearance.

My first choice for roasting, on a less lavish scale than sirloin or standing ribs, would be a rolled roast from either of these prime cuts. A particularly nice-looking roast is the French *contre filet*, or *faux filet*, from the short loin, boned top of sirloin or the whole sirloin strip, trimmed and tied to give a neat, compact shape, ideal for carving. Whenever possible, meat should be cooked on the bone, which contributes both fat and flavor. In the case of beef, however, this is only possible on a very large scale, as a rib roast consisting of two bones would be thin and dry. An American friend compromises by getting the butcher to bone and roll the meat, then to tie it back on the bone. In this way he feels that he retains some of the benefits, yet he has at the end, after easily removing the bone, a compact roast, which is easy to carve.

Many of the old English beef dishes are rarely seen nowadays; some of them are well worth reviving. One is "beef olives": thin slices of tender beef beaten out even thinner with a mallet, then rolled around small handfuls of bread and onion stuffing, flavored with herbs. They are neatly tied with string, then braised with carrots and onions in a meat gravy, and usually served on a bed of mashed potatoes. Steak and kidney pudding is another good old-fashioned dish; it is excellent on a cold winter's day. A lighter version is the lesser known and strangely named "sea pie," which consists of stewed beef with onions and carrots topped with a crisp lid of pastry.

A popular dish in London gentlemen's clubs used to be marrow bones; the cut ends were sealed with pastry, and the bones were boiled standing upright and served wrapped in a napkin. The marrow was extracted by each diner, armed with a narrow silver spoon, and eaten with toast. Marrow bones can often be had for the asking. This is an amazing giveaway of precious material, for beef marrow is the richest and most easily digested of all fats, perfect for feeding invalids and children. It adds succulence to a risotto, or can be made into delicate dumplings mixed with chopped herbs. Alternatively, it can be used as the fat, for frying onions, or making stews.

In terms of food values, beef is by far the most valuable of meats. It is richer in protein and minerals than mutton, the only comparable mature meat, which is practically nonexistent nowadays even in Britain; very much richer in iron, calcium and vitamin B than lamb or veal; and richer than pork in calcium and iron.

20

The bountiful pig

The pig provides us with a wider range of food than any other animal—spicy sausages, pâtés, smoked hams, succulent roasts and much more besides

The pig is without doubt the most versatile of all animals from the cook's point of view. Almost every part can be eaten, from the nose to the tail, although I would rather not have to put that to the test. Its snout, cheeks, ears, heart, intestines, liver, tongue, brains, kidneys, feet, tail and even its testicles are all highly prized by some people. It also gives excellent fat and a very tasty skin.

Apart from these side products, the best cuts of the pig are highly adaptable and can be prepared in a number of ways, according to regional tastes. These include salting, or pickling in brine; smoking; salting and smoking; preserving, as in *confit de porc*; and cooking fresh. Thus it gives an enormous range of sausages, both smoked and fresh; bacon, smoked and sweet-cured; and many different hams, from the strongly flavored raw smoked ones to the milder ones which are cured but not smoked, and are to be boiled or baked. Pork fat is useful in various different forms: the solid back fat, which can be bought from some butchers for adding to pâtés; and melted fat or lard.

Each country has different priorities: in England there is a wide choice of good hams, gammons (front legs or the top of ham off hind legs) and sausages. In Italy the first preference is toward raw smoked delicacies, such as Parma ham and salamis. The French have a vast range of *charcuterie*, many different sausages, both smoked and fresh, and countless pâtés. In the United States, with its diversity of peoples, one can obtain almost all these things, but England is the only country I know lucky enough to get the skin (for crackling) along with the fat on roast pork (although now Americans can buy it specially, from Chinese shops). In France they pare away most of the fat, leaving only enough to enclose the meat, and the *bardes* of fat are sold separately, as is the skin.

Pig's feet are fairly easy to come by, and I find them invaluable. They can be eaten either cold, in a vinaigrette, or hot: boiled, coated with bread crumbs, broiled, and served with a mustard sauce. With their highly gelatinous quality, they cannot be improved upon for making a good natural *gelée* (particularly when combined with knuckle of veal). Spareribs are one of my favorite treats. They are not too expensive, but are more bone than meat: as a main course one should allow a full pound per person. They can be troublesome to cook indoors in large quantities, but are ideal for a barbecue.

Pork is important in Chinese cooking, and its bland flesh goes exceptionally well with sweet and sour combinations, and with spicy flavors.

Some butchers sell ground pork, and I find this useful for making stuffings for poultry and for meat balls and dishes like stuffed cabbage. A whole suckling pig is something I have yet to experience. Much as I love all forms of ham, bacon, salami and sausages, I am too squeamish a cook to relish making things like brawn or head cheese—the very words make me blanch. So for these and other dishes of this sort I rely on good *charcuteries*, with their appetizing arrays of *crépinettes*, *andouillettes*, *boudins noirs et blancs*, *museau de tête* and *pieds de porc vinaigrette*, as well as a variety of sausages both smoked and fresh, and excellent pure pork pâtés.

1 *Pure pork chipolata sausages*
2 *Boudin blanc*
3 *Saucisse de Toulouse*
4 *Boudin noir*
5 *Saucisson sec*
6 *Pork fillets in cider sauce*
7 *Sausage roll*
8 *Bacon*
9 *Pork chops with juniper berries*
10 *Breaded pigs' feet*
11 *Pork pie*
12 *Spareribs in barbecue sauce*
13 *Gammon*

The surprising sausage

From the spicy, smoked salamis of Eastern Europe to the ubiquitous frankfurter, the sausage, whatever the size or shape, is a favorite item in every cuisine

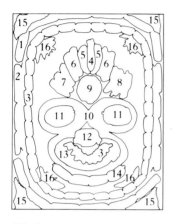

1 Beef sausages
2 Pork chipolatas
3 Pork cocktail sausages
4 Algerian merguez
5 Auvergne fumées
6 Toulouse sausages
7 Saucisson Mont Belliard
8 Italian salamelles
9 English black pudding
10 French boudin noir
11 Boudin blanc, parsley
12 Scottish haggis
13 German bockwurst
14 German knackwurst
15 Parsley
16 Sage and thyme

Sausages are an ancient form of food; they were much prized by the Romans for whom pork was a favorite meat. Their sausages were probably heavily cured by smoking or salting; for them the sausage was a means of preserving those parts of the pig which were not suitable for roasting. The art of smoking sausages is one that the Italians have excelled at ever since. Apart from the salamis which are cured for so long that they are eaten uncooked, the majority of Italian sausages are now lightly salted or smoked, which adds to the flavor and acts as a slight preservative. Some of the best come from the Romagna area around Bologna. In Modena they make the *cotechino*, a large sausage of pure pork lightly salted, weighing from one to two pounds. Cooked by long simmering, it is one of the traditional ingredients of *bollito misto*. The *zampone*, also made in Modena, consists of a similar filling encased in the skin of a pig's foot. The fresh sausages of this region, called *salciccia* to distinguish them from the smoked *salamelle*, are also very good, similar to French *saucisses de Toulouse*, coarsely cut and highly seasoned.

In France there is an even greater number of lightly smoked or salted sausage, quite apart from the *saucissons secs*, which can, indeed must, be kept for five or six months before being eaten raw, like the *saucisson à l'ail*. The semi-cured varieties vary greatly according to the region; some, like the little *saucissons d'Arles*, can be eaten raw or cooked. Others, like the more heavily smoked *saucisses de Francfort*, need only to be heated, while the *saucisses de Toulouse* need thorough cooking. A coarse garlic-flavored boiling sausage of about ¾ lb is ideal for adding to a cassoulet, or for serving with hot potato salad, haricot beans, chick peas or lentils. These make hearty meals, perfect for cold weather; but they are not for those with weak digestions.

In Spain a coarse sausage of the *chorizo* type, highly seasoned with garlic and hot peppers, is often cooked in stews or added to soups. In Germany and other central European countries the sausages have a different character; they tend to be smoother in consistency, firm and quite highly smoked. These, the many different types of wurst, go exceptionally well with dishes of sauerkraut, and red and white cabbage. Another I particularly like is the Polish *kabanos*; a small spicy sausage, it can be eaten raw with salads,

heated and served with lentils or sliced for pizzas.

Similar to sausage is the black pudding, or *boudin*, found in almost every European country in some form. Unlike the English one, which is bland in flavor, almost sweet, the continental ones are well flavored with onion. The white pudding, or *boudin blanc*, is more delicate. The French ones are usually made from a mixture of white chicken, pork or veal, and eggs; those made in the north of England and Scotland are composed largely of oatmeal mixed with suet, chopped onion and black pepper. Similar in content is the Scottish haggis, made from coarse oatmeal mixed with sheep's lungs, heart and liver, chopped onion, suet and spices. The whole is enclosed in a sheep's stomach and boiled gently for one to two hours, depending on size. It can be surprisingly good, cut in slices and served with sauce made from thin cream flavored to taste with meat extract and Scotch whisky.

For those who have the time, I recommend making one's own sausages. This is neither difficult nor complicated, so long as one has the necessary aids. Some mixers have sausage-making attachments, and sausage casings are now available by mail order. Originally made from the intestines of the pigs—on average each pig has from fifty to sixty feet of small intestine—these casings are now mostly made from sheep's stomachs. A food processor is useful for making the filling, since it allows one to vary the texture according to taste, but good sausages can be made perfectly well with a grinder. I have made seven different fillings and they have all been good. Probably the best was a pork sausage, quite coarsely cut and highly seasoned with garlic, juniper berries, salt and very coarsely ground black pepper. In the summer I add fresh basil and parsley, in winter a little fresh sage and parsley. I have also used mixtures of beef and pork, venison, veal and rabbit; whatever mixture of meat one uses, the proportions should be roughly two parts lean meat to one of hard fat. The best fat is the hard back fat of the pig, called fatback in the United States. Many American supermarkets have it, but few butcher shops; instead, one can use a fairly fat cut, like belly of pork, and mix it with an equal amount of lean meat. Freshly made sausages are a beautiful sight, with a marblelike mosaic of pink, green and white shining through their translucent skins.

New World cuisine

Shaking off the strictures of the Old World, the New England settlers evolved a cooking style of their own based on native resources and epitomized by the Thanksgiving dinner

Although the turkey is traditionally eaten at Christmas throughout the United States as in Great Britain, its true place in American cuisine is at Thanksgiving. Held on the fourth Thursday in November, the feast commemorates the landing of the Pilgrim Fathers in 1620, and the foods appropriate to it are the foods that the newcomers found in the New World: the turkey itself, corn, sweet potato, squash, cranberry and pumpkin. They are symbolic of native American foods, and the holiday also serves as a rough equivalent to the British harvest festival. The turkey itself is native to Central and North America, and the Indians had already started to domesticate it by the time of the arrival of the *Mayflower*. Wild turkeys still exist in some parts of the country and are said to be superior in flavor to the domestic bird. Corn was the basic food of the Indians; they discovered it growing wild in the Mexican highlands, and started to cultivate it. They made it into corn bread, hominy and succotash—a true Indian word. Corn may make its appearance along with the turkey on the Thanksgiving table, in chowder as a first course, as fritters, or in bread or stuffing. Yams and sweet potatoes were also among the Indians' basic foods, and they too still form a part of the annual Thanksgiving dinner, usually candied, and sometimes even topped with sticky marshmallows.

Squash is another indigenous food, of which there are literally dozens of different varieties in America, from the soft-skinned summer squashes which must be eaten soon after harvesting to the hard-skinned winter squashes which can be stored for months. The pumpkin, another native food, is almost invariably made into a sweet pie that is served as a dessert.

The settlers also found a rich variety of wild game, birds and fish, beans, peas, melons, and edible seeds, nuts and roots. Year by year the New England cuisine developed; then for 200 years it changed little. By the nineteenth century, the Americans' food had become more refined without losing its basic simplicity. A typical supper might consist of fried ham, baked beans in chili sauce and johnnycake, with sour cream pie and Dutch cheese to follow. A more elaborate dinner, on Sundays, might be fricassee of chicken with hot biscuits and gravy, mashed potatoes and boiled onions. In the summer, communal meals were sometimes eaten outdoors; perhaps a whole ham simmered in cider with a handful of raisins, then covered in a crust of brown sugar and mustard, and baked until golden brown; huge pots of beans cooked a long time with salt pork; platters of cold chicken and hard-boiled eggs, accompanied by pickled beets, homemade chili sauce, and freshly baked bread. For dessert, there would be an array of frosted layer cakes oozing cream. Another of these open-air meals was the corn roast, somewhat like an inland version of a clambake. Great numbers of corn cobs and potatoes would be buried in a pit of smoldering coals to roast, and then be eaten with fried chicken, and watermelon to follow. When I think of American food, this is the sort of cooking that comes to mind: simple and delicious dishes cooked in ways that evolved from local resources.

In some respects American food has stayed closer to the English Elizabethan table than our own (that is, food of the northeastern seaboard which was settled by the English, for of course other immigrants to other parts of the country brought specialties with them, all of which have influenced the cuisines of the nation as a whole). If you compare a list of classic American dishes with an English cookbook of the sixteenth century, you cannot fail to be struck by the similarities. The cheesecake is a very close relative of the "loaves of cheese curds" so often found in books of the Stuart period; pumpkin pie is very like the many sweet vegetable tarts that were common at that time; cinnamon toast was an old English treat that has since been forgotten in England, as was hot spiced wine, still served at American hunt breakfasts. Mincemeat in America is still often made in the old English way, to include minced beefsteak—a custom not practiced in Great Britain for hundreds of years. Indeed, until 1878 the English and American pint were the same size; it was the English measure that changed, so that the United States measures are in fact truer to early English recipes than are the English ones.

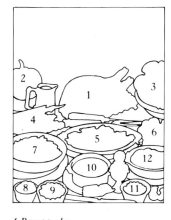

1 Roast turkey
2 Pumpkin
3 Varied squash
4 Freshly picked sweet corn
5 Corn fritters
6 Hot cloverleaf rolls
7 Wild rice with onions and almonds
8 Pumpkin puree
9 Blueberries
10 Corn chowder, soda crackers
11 Cranberry sauce
12 Candied sweet potatoes

Goose and duck

Dark, succulent and crisply browned, this brace of birds, served hot or cold with a feast of different vegetables and special sauces, will grace any festive table

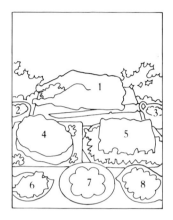

1 Roast goose
2 Cranberry sauce
3 Applesauce
4 Duck and chicken in aspic
5 Duck pâté
6 Bacon rolls
7 Forcemeat balls
8 Chipolata sausages

Although in its culinary aspect the goose is firmly rooted in France and its cuisine, in its live form I connect it vividly with the English rural scene: the village green with geese waddling and honking around the pond, or the farmyard where geese and ducks together scrabble for grain. I have never thought of it as a culinary creature, but more as something figuring in myths or fairy tales. I suppose I have, over a period of years, eaten goose in various forms. But until recently I had never actually cooked a goose.

The English goose is a very different creature from the French one, which has been artificially fattened to such a degree that a bird can yield as much as two and a half pounds of fat, and its liver may weigh as much as two pounds or even more, perhaps a quarter the weight of the whole bird. One must adapt French recipes accordingly: a *confit d'oie*, for example, can only be made outside France by adding a large proportion of pork fat to the goose's fat; and a pâté of goose liver is out of the question, although its liver can, with advantage, be added to a pâté mixture. In France, *confit d'oie* was never eaten straight away, or all at once, but used gradually during the lean winter months between Christmas and Easter, hot or cold, in soups or stews, as an improvement to other dishes rather than a dish in itself. Some of the fat would be stored and used instead of pork fat, beef drippings, butter or olive oil. This delicate fat, the best of all in my opinion, gives the cooking of certain regions of France a special character all its own.

In England in times past, a goose would be killed for a special occasion like a wedding or a family reunion; the bird would be eaten at one meal, and the residue of fat carefully stored and kept for many uses, few of them related to the kitchen. (Goose grease was used in poultices, for the softening of stiffened leather, oiling of dairy churns, and polishing of horses' hooves before a show, among other things.) A goose is still killed and eaten occasionally in rural England, usually at Michaelmas or at Christmas; but in most places the turkey has usurped its popularity.

The first goose I ever cooked was so delicious, particularly when cold, that I would highly recommend it for any festive occasion, served cold with a choice of sauces and salads. I feel instinctively that goose is better not stuffed, for this allows more fat to escape. But many people would prefer it hot, and would consider stuffing an essential. Perhaps a very plain stuffing is the answer: cored and quartered apples, for instance, or boiled chestnuts, or sliced boiled onions; or a celery and bread crumb mixture or an excellent one based on mashed potatoes. A large amount of stuffing is needed, for the goose, like the duck, is a hollow bird with a shallow breast. The traditional English accompaniment to a goose at Christmas would be applesauce, onion sauce, or bread sauce; but I prefer a sauce of horseradish and apples, or a cranberry sauce which goes well with all poultry and game. Both are equally good with a hot or cold bird. With the hot goose I would serve roast potatoes; although rich, they are so delicious when cooked in the goose fat that they are irresistible. And for a vegetable I would make red cabbage the day before and reheat it on the day. For a meal at any other time besides Christmas, when a certain degree of conventionality seems appropriate, I would serve *kasha* (buckwheat) with just a green salad. *Kasha* is the old Russian accompaniment for goose, and is delicious either as a side dish or as a stuffing. Sauerkraut is also good with goose and can double as stuffing. With a cold roast goose I would serve a hot puree of potatoes and two salads: one of beets, endive and watercress, the other of romaine lettuce, green pepper, avocado and segments of orange.

Duck is similar to goose, with its crisp brown skin and dark tasty flesh, but is considerably smaller. With a good rice stuffing, an applesauce flavored with orange juice, a creamy dish of mashed potatoes and a green vegetable, and with a watercress and orange salad on the side, it will make a festive meal for two. A fruit sauce served with it makes it even more unusual: Cumberland sauce, or one made from cherries or plums.

Duck can also give a valuable amount of first-rate fat, plus liver for adding to a pâté, and an excellent stock, perhaps for a really good onion soup. A useful dish for post-Christmas meals is a cold duck in aspic, or it can be made, as here, with duck and chicken in alternate layers.

Game birds

The traditional roasting and serving of game birds with all the last-minute chores is a daunting task; braising is a simpler and more flexible alternative

I have felt for some time that there are two distinctly opposed forms of cooking—in English cooking, at least, if not in every cuisine. One is that practiced by good restaurants, with chefs and sous-chefs, numerous helpers, and batteries of saucepans keeping hot in *bains-marie*, while the other is more appropriate to home cooks. There might almost be a third subdivision for the few families who still employ a cook, for on the whole it is the limitation placed on the home cook who must both prepare the food and eat it, which separates the amateurs from the professionals. There are a few occasions when I prepare a meal for just one solitary friend and I can indulge in dishes such as fritters which are eaten as they come from the pan; but even then I resent not being able to give my whole attention to either the friend or the food, and both inevitably suffer.

This belief holds particularly true when applied to game cookery. Few things are more delicious than a perfectly roasted bird, hung to the right degree and roasted to the minute, served with French fried potatoes, gravy and bread sauce. But for a home cook to attempt this is over-ambitious, and I have given up trying. Instead I have evolved a new system of cooking game which I find almost as delicious and half as much work. It is quite simply to braise rather than roast. In the past, I have been put off braised game because only old birds were considered suitable for this treatment. But I find that young birds respond excellently to braising, and this way you also avoid the danger of dryness, which occasionally results from roasting a bird, especially pheasant. A further advantage is that the time is not so vital as in roasting; the dish can be kept hot for an extra half hour without fear of its being spoiled by drying out.

My recipe for braised game can be used for any bird; I have used it with pheasant, grouse, partridge, pigeons, and even guinea fowl, all with excellent results. The accompaniments to braised game are quite different from the usual ones for roast game, and are less time-consuming and worrying. Instead of gravy and bread sauce, a simple sauce made from the cooking liquor enriched with sour cream can be made quickly. Celery or red cabbage, my two favorite vegetable accompaniments for game, can be braised in the oven at the same time as the birds. All the other autumn vegetables—leeks, onions, fennel, white cabbage—are also good braised with the game. Root vegetables have a special affinity to game, and a mixture of carrots, parsnips and turnips, softened in game fat and then gently stewed in its stock, cannot be improved upon as a vegetable dish to accompany game.

Chestnuts are another particularly appropriate accompaniment, but I would only plan on these if I knew I would have the time and energy (or an assistant) for the shelling, for chestnuts out of a can are just not the same thing. A thin puree of potatoes, or pieces of bread fried golden in drippings, can complete the main course. Another point in favor of braising is that the remains will make a wonderful soup, combining the flavors of the bird with those of the braised vegetables, and you can add any remaining sauce to the soup as well.

I consider lentils and game an excellent combination, and I frequently make a soup using these two together. A stock made from game is the best stock of all for vegetable soups, transforming them from light summer dishes to warming and sustaining cold-weather foods. Even quite ordinary soups like those made from onion, beans or beets (borsch) have a whole new potential when made with game stock. A strained game stock, well reduced and seasoned, also makes a first-rate consommé.

Old game birds are rarely seen nowadays in the shops, but when I do come across one I buy it and make pâtés with the best of the meat, and a soup with all the remainder. The braising recipe can, if desired, be adapted for old birds by extending the cooking time, but I prefer to use them in these other ways. I find my pressure cooker is an extremely good way of cooking tough old birds; they respond well to being cooked under pressure, and much precious time is saved, as well as fuel.

I only cook game two or three times a year, so I have refined my list of favorite game recipes down to a very few. I like to vary a good recipe by using different birds, perhaps substituting partridges for the more usual pheasant. The soup, of course, also varies with the choice of bird and vegetables, and the character of the pâtés alters completely, depending on which variety of bird and which wine and seasonings are used.

1 Cold game pie
2 Game pâté with chestnuts
3 Game soup with lentils
4 Game pie
5 Buckwheat with vegetables
6 Small game pies
7 Cumberland sauce
8 Whole grain mustard

_H_andsome pies

Rediscover the great pleasures of baking day and make a batch of delicious and sustaining pies to share with friends or freeze for future unexpected occasions

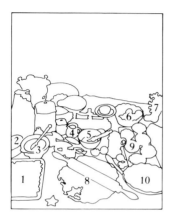

1 _Poached chicken, precooked vegetables for chicken pie_
2 _Butter_
3 _White sauce with parsley_
4 _Cream_
5 _Egg yolk_
6 _Eggs_
7 _Parsley_
8 _Pastry dough_
9 _Small meat pies_
10 _Rabbit pie_

tomato and mustard
  quiches p73
small game pies p84

A temporary shortage of money in one's pocket can be a real advantage, paradoxically, for some cooks; and I am one of them. I find I work best within limitations, whether imposed by lack of cash or of materials. It is in times of comparative affluence that I start to panic. When the affluence is on a national scale, I start to feel that people's standards have become too high, that we have been spoiled by too-elegant restaurant meals and too many dinner invitations. I remember hearing a fellow guest at a dinner party complain that he could not face another salmon; and hearing someone else recommend a _filet de boeuf en croûte_ as ideal picnic food. In this sort of atmosphere I quickly become defeatist; when absolutely anything is within the bounds of possibility, nothing seems good enough.

Until recently many of us were still trying to live according to a pattern laid down by our grandparents in an era of prosperity, living in large houses without the servants that were an integral consideration in the original plans for the house, giving dinner parties that would in previous times have kept a staff of two or three fully occupied for a couple of days; in short, we were trying to keep jobs, bring up children, run houses, maintain gardens, and entertain in a way that was far too demanding for most of us to accomplish without a degree of strain. I find it a relief that the economic realities of recent times have forced us to abandon all this, and find a simpler way of living, more within our reach.

In my house, at any rate, the planning of large dinner parties has become a thing of the past; so long past, in fact, that it has almost faded into myth. With handicaps such as lack of time, money, help, and inclination, I even hesitate to

commit myself to any culinary effort more than a couple of days in advance. Rather than organizing dinner parties one simply asks friends in for a meal. This informality means a much less rigorous menu; one hot dish is really all that is needed, although more can of course be added, as you feel inclined. I like savory pies for this sort of meal, as they are a good example of a dish that can stand alone. A large meat pie is a handsome thing, and quite delicious and sustaining enough to form the basis of a meal. These pies are also adaptable, to feed an indefinite number of people, and the main ingredient can be chosen from a wide range of food, from quails stuffed with pâté to the humble rabbit.

However busy I am, I am determined not to give up cooking for pleasure; one mustn't lose sight of the fact that both cooking and eating are enjoyable activities. I try to keep an afternoon free for just truly relaxed cooking at least twice a month—not in the old hectic rush of preparing for one special meal, but in a quieter, calmer way, making a series of related dishes for future use. The old-fashioned system of having a special "day" for baking, for instance, was a sound idea that still makes sense, economically and practically. With two or three pounds of pastry, one can make a series of pies, tarts and linings for quiches. One of these can be eaten the same day and the others frozen for future meals.

Particularly with a modern freezer at hand, it is a lovely feeling to have more food than one actually needs at any given time; and is a perfect incentive to telephone friends and invite them over. Viewed in this way, cooking becomes enjoyable again; the pleasure of doing things for fun rather than necessity is regained.

One-pot cooking

A range of different ingredients cooked together makes for a wonderful mingling of flavors and is a highly practical, economical and energy-saving way to entertain

My idea of a perfect meal has changed. It used to be a selection of different foods—meat or fish, vegetables and sauces—all cooked separately and meeting for the first time on my plate. I still think this can be delicious, but I realize how wasteful it is in terms of pots and pans, fuel and labor. As far as home cooking is concerned, I have now swung to the opposite extreme, which is both more practical and more economical. In this system, a group of different foods is cooked together, each adding its flavors to the others and the separate ingredients merging into a whole.

Almost every country has its own version of a "one-pot" meal: New England boiled dinner, Scottish cock-a-leekie, French pot-au-feu, Italian *bollito misto*, Moroccan couscous. Some of these dishes require special equipment, but in most cases one can devise one's own version with a little ingenuity.

Before the days of kitchen ranges, when cooking was still done over the open fire, whole meals were cooked in one huge pot, or cauldron. I used to think that this contained one vast watery stew, or a large cut of meat boiling in gallons of water, but I was wrong. Apparently as many as six or seven different foods were often cooked at one time, by an ingenious method of coordination. Inside the giant pot a flat plank of wood would be wedged near the bottom, and under this a piece of meat—probably ham or salt beef—would cook, while on top of the board would be two or three earthenware jars, tightly sealed. Inside these might be found meat combined with root vegetables for soups or stews, eggs in the shell and cut-up chickens. In a muslin bag hanging from the handle, some dried vegetables or a pudding might be steaming. By careful timing, all these foods could be combined to provide quite elaborate meals.

A similar method was used by the "bargees," or bargemen, who used to cook their dinner in an iron bucket over a fire on the towpath alongside the river or canal. Inside the bucket, on a platform of sticks or flat stones, would stand a large earthenware jar, probably filled with a mixture of meat and vegetables, and perhaps suet dumplings, tightly sealed with a flour and water paste. Also in the bucket might be a pudding in a bag, or simply a bottle of tea.

In modern times, with our efficient electric and gas ovens with pre-set timers, one-pot meals are more apt to be in the form of baked casseroles than pots of boiled food. The word casserole originally meant the pot in which the food was cooked; now it has come to mean the food itself. Casseroles range from traditional meat stews—*daubes* of beef, *navarins* of lamb, cassoulet, moussaka, Lancashire hotpot—to combinations of vegetables.

Hearty and delicious dishes can be made by using layers of different foods: at the bottom goes a layer of cooked rice, buckwheat or couscous, then various uncooked vegetables, usually moistened with a sauce. Over it all goes a covering of dried bread, grated cheese, or bread crumbs. Alternatively, all three layers can be of vegetables, the top layer a puree of potatoes, celeriac, parsnips or turnips, or a mixture.

These inexpensive and heartening dishes are eminently suitable for life today; the work of preparing them can be done in advance, and the final cooking done in the oven, possibly preset, or even over the fire. Many of us these days have friends who are vegetarian, and it is not always easy for nonvegetarians to think of a filling meal without using meat. These sorts of dishes need only a green salad and bread as accompaniment, and can be kept hot indefinitely.

1 The "bargee's" meat and vegetables
2 Steamed pudding

Cooking round the hearth

Gather the family around an open fire to enjoy the crackling, sizzling and bubbling and the delicious aroma of food cooking to perfection in the roaring flames

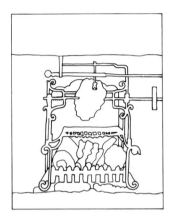

A baron of beef on a spit over an open fire

fireplace-grilled fish p74
fireplace-grilled
  chicken p81

I read recently the fascinating fact that until 1850 all the cooking for the White House was carried out in two huge open fireplaces. The old chef was said to be hostile toward the new range installed in that year—perhaps understandably, since he had been accustomed for many years to cooking grand dinners for as many as thirty-six people without it.

Cooking over a fire has always appealed to Americans, who have a gift for simple living combined with a degree of comfort (something the more puritan English have never quite understood). In 1939, when King George VI and his Queen visited the United States, President Franklin D. Roosevelt held a huge informal picnic in their honor at the Roosevelts' Hyde Park estate at which much of the food was cooked over an enormous open fire.

Richard Olney, in his book *The French Menu Cookbook* gives detailed drawings of the fireplace in his house in the South of France built expressly for cooking. Here he roasts and broils meats, bakes vegetables in the ashes, and smokes food in the chimney.

I once visited some friends who were living in a tiny cottage on the side of a mountain in County Kerry. For three years the wife had been doing all the cooking for her husband and two small children—and all the heating of water—in the fireplace. She had been lucky enough to find the cottage still equipped with its original fireplace crane in good working order, and by scouring junk shops and markets far and wide, she had acquired a complete set of authentic old pots and pans, plus the hooks from which they hang. A friendly blacksmith had made her a trivet by welding three horseshoes together and attaching legs to them. This would support flat pans like skillets directly over the fire. Thus equipped, there was literally no cooking she could not manage to do. An excellent and inventive cook, she made soups and stews, and cooked fresh and dried vegetables and grains; pot-roasted rabbits, hares, chickens, deer and even kid; made flat bread like *chapatis* on a griddle; and baked yeasted bread and cakes in an Irish version of what we usually call a Dutch oven.

The day I visited them was a typically Irish day of the worst sort: grey and drizzling. The small living room was both lit and warmed by the fire in its huge chimney breast, seemingly out of all proportion to the size of the room, but with reason. For it was the hub of all activity. A stew was cooking over the fire for lunch, bread was slowly rising at the edge of the fire, damp clothes were hung over the end of the crane, a kettle hung nearby, permanently on the verge of boiling, and the cat lay asleep on the hearth.

Despite the inconveniences, and they are many, there is something very appealing to me in this sort of life, although I am sure I would not have the stamina to endure it day in and day out. The main disadvantage is the black greasy skin the flames produce on the outside of the cooking pots; even with plenty of hot water, they are very hard to clean. The main benefit is that it brings cooking back into the heart of family life. Rather than the mother working alone in the kitchen, other members of the family are drawn in, and can help in positive ways. Even quite young children, who might be confused or misled by many modern refinements like pressure cookers or microwave ovens, understand and respect the heat of a blazing fireplace.

The age-old device of the crane, the iron bar hanging within the chimney breast high over the fire, on a swivel so that it can be swung away from the fire when desired, combined with the varying length of the different hooks, gives a surprising degree of heat control. As well as the pots which hang from the crane, which include a cauldron for heating large amounts of water, a kettle, and different-sized lidded pots, there are a number of flat pans like skillets and griddles for standing on trivets, and the sort of Dutch oven called a bastable. This, the traditional baking pot of Wales and Ireland, is shaped like a modern French casserole with the addition of three short legs for standing among the hot ashes, and a flat lid. On this lid are piled red-hot peats; this creates the even heat of an oven.

The only modern invention I can think of which adds to the possibilities of open-fire cookery is aluminum foil. This, especially the heavy-duty, can be used in countless ways: pieces of meat, poultry or fish can be wrapped alone or with garnishes of vegetables and baked in the ashes or over the fire on a grill; whole vegetables can be wrapped and baked in the ashes; foil-wrapped eggs can be baked in the shell; shellfish can be wrapped and steamed; and whole apples can be sugared and then baked in foil.

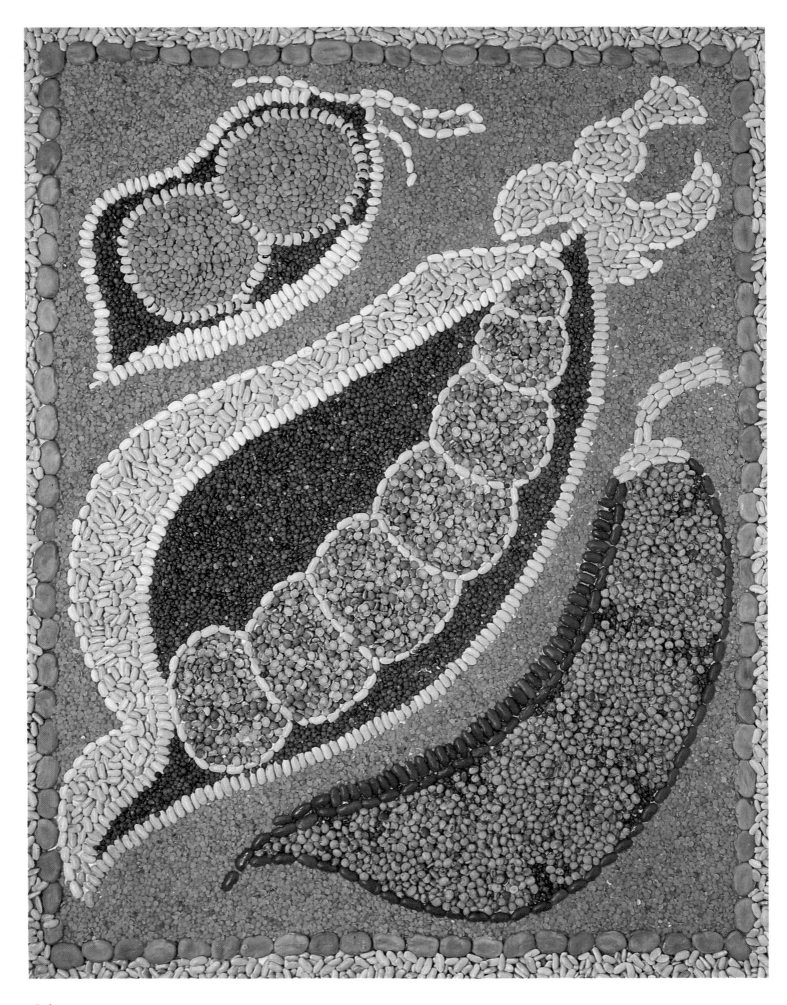

Dried peas and beans

From Mexico to Morocco, almost every country has a national dish based on dried peas or beans that is restoring, comforting and packed with real goodness

In the winter months when one reaches home cold and tired at the end of the day, one yearns for food as an antidote to chills and fatigue. The French rarely eat cold food, especially in the evening, avoiding what they call *froid à l'estomac*. At this time what one needs is warming food— not merely served hot, but food with a comforting quality. Lentils rate high on my list, for there is something essentially restoring about them. Hot, semi-liquid, easily digested, full of iron and vitamins, they are a perfect example of the best sort of winter food.

My favorite dish of this sort is "Esau's potage," a Middle Eastern stew of lentils and rice, supposedly the very "mess of pottage" which induced Esau to sell his birthright. Split pea soup is also a good restorer. Dried beans in general provide a wide range of sustaining and nourishing dishes for cold weather, while in the summer months they can be made into delicious vinaigrettes and salads, or even smooth pastes that are good spread on hot bread.

I believe that all dried vegetables should have a measure of fat or oil added at some stage, to counteract their very dryness. Animal fats are particularly good used in this way; a piece of beef marrow stirred into freshly boiled haricot or navy beans will make the beans into a rich luxurious dish. In summer if they are to be at room temperature—they should never be eaten chilled—they should first be well moistened with the best olive oil, cut with a little white wine vinegar or lemon juice. Apart from split peas, all my favorite varieties of dried legumes come from the continent. I like the French *soisson*, a medium-size white kidney-shaped bean, and the Italian *cannellini*, which is very similar. I also love the pale green dried *flageolets* and the dark red

kidney bean. These three can be mixed together in a well-flavored vinaigrette to make a pretty tri-colored dish. I like the so-called brown lentil from the continent (actually dull olive green) and the rare green lentil, generally prized above all others. There are many beautiful varieties of beans, ranging from warm chestnut browns to a pale cream color.

Almost every country has a national dish based on some form of dried bean or pea. The English have pease pudding and pea soup; Americans have Boston baked beans; the Mexicans have black beans; in India it is *dhal*, in Egypt *ful medames*, the Arabs eat *hummus*, and in Spain there are many dishes of *garbanzos* (chick peas). It seems, moreover, that some day we will all come to rely at least in part on soy beans, as these most nutritious and easily grown of foods contain vast amounts of minerals and vitamins. They can be treated in exactly the same way as the navy beans, soaked and cooked slowly, with plenty of fat and salt and pepper added, and served hot; or they can be served cool, in a vinaigrette made of lots of good olive oil and vinegar, chopped raw onion, parsley and garlic, salt and pepper.

Another dried legume to consider is the small *azuki* bean, which grows in China and Japan. Although tiny, it takes as long to cook as other larger beans. The chick pea, familiar in Spain, is also part of the staple diet throughout the Middle East, in Morocco and parts of France and Italy. They are an acquired taste, but once one has grown to like them, they can become a real passion. I like them best made into *hummus*: mixed to a smooth paste with *tahini* (sesame seed paste), lemon juice and garlic. They also make good soups, and they are one of the essential ingredients of a genuine couscous.

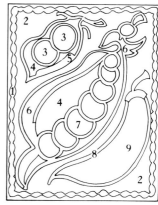

1 *Dried broad beans*
2 *Red lentils*
3 *Brown lentils bordered by black-eyed peas*
4 *Black lentils*
5 *Haricots blancs*
6 *Green flageolets*
7 *Split peas*
8 *Red kidney beans*
9 *Haricots roses and black lentils*

Root vegetables

An obstinate refusal to submit graciously to canning or freezing, and an apparent determination to remain unfashionable, endears root vegetables to lovers of fresh food

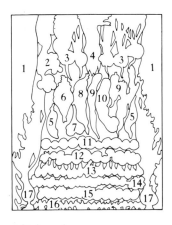

For some years now I have been growing steadily more attached to root vegetables—I mean such things as turnips, beets, parsnips, carrots and Jerusalem artichokes. They seem determinedly unfashionable, which is one reason I love them; totally resistant to modern times, they cannot be frozen or canned successfully, and the best way to store them is still to dig a pit underground, as our ancestors used to do.

More unusual root vegetables—salsify, scorzonera (oyster plant), celeriac (celery root), kohlrabi and fennel—seem scarcely more popular. It takes imagination, certainly, to visualize these ugly swollen tubers as smooth soups and elegant purees. Perhaps the trouble is that root vegetables are rarely sold young enough to be at their best. Those people lucky enough to have their own gardens soon discover the virtues of gathering them while still quite small, for it is then that they are at their most versatile. Many are delicious eaten raw, like radishes. Turnips, celeriac and kohlrabi are all unusually good cut in slices, chilled and served on a platter of crudités. When picked at this stage, their leaves can be cooked separately as a green vegetable. Turnips can also be left in the ground all winter to yield a crop of green leaves for use in early spring.

It has become fashionable in France recently to serve a selection of two or three vegetable purees with a meat dish, and root vegetables are ideal for this. A puree of Jerusalem artichokes makes a delicious accompaniment to steaks, and a celeriac puree is excellent with game or poultry. A puree of turnips is good with lamb; a mixture of carrots and turnips goes well with veal or pork. When serving two or three purees at the same time, they should not all be of root vegetables, obviously, for this would be monotonous. A puree of green beans would be delicious with one of parsnips and another of mushrooms, served with ham. A green pea puree would be good with one of celeriac and a third one of broccoli to accompany a roast capon. The purees should be well seasoned and blended until they are very smooth, almost like thick sauces.

One of the reasons root vegetables are not more popular may be due to our insistence on eating potatoes with every meat dish, for they do not go well with potatoes, themselves a root crop. A proportion of potato, however, can with advantage be mixed with the other root vegetable, for this helps give a firm dry puree; one made of parsnips and potato, for example, makes a delicious accompaniment to broiled steaks, with the pan juices scraped and poured over it. A puree of celeriac and potato makes a good "bed" for poached eggs: sprinkle them with grated cheese and brown in the broiler before serving.

These same purees, thinned with stock or milk, constitute excellent soups. The vegetables provide all that a soup requires in terms of flavor, nourishment, texture and color, so nothing need be added beyond perhaps a sprinkling of chopped parsley. In combining them, I particularly like beet with fennel, turnip with carrot and parsnip, carrot with celeriac. They are best of all made with a good game or beef stock, for they have a special affinity with strong meaty flavors. For the same reason they should be sautéed whenever possible in animal fat; beef drippings, goose or duck fat are ideal for the purpose. Remember that they are highly absorbent, and must not be allowed to retain water; for this reason, after boiling, they should be well dried out, in a warm oven, and then given plenty of butter.

40

$\mathcal{A}$ feast of potatoes

The humble potato, whether transformed into pancakes, soufflés, gnocchi, bread, scones or cakes, or simply boiled in its skin is the perfect foil for meat, poultry and fish

Anyone who has not visited Britain cannot know just how good potatoes can be. Of all the basic starchy foods—bread, rice, pasta and potatoes—I think I like potatoes best. Irish potatoes have always seemed the finest of all to me, although those grown in Wales are also very delicious. Not only do they grow well in our temperate climate, they also seem ideally suited to eating on damp winter days, being warming and sustaining in nature and valuable in vitamins as well, so long as they are cooked correctly. The vitamin content lies largely in the skin, or just below it, so that whenever possible potatoes should be eaten in their skins; or if peeled, this should be done after cooking. Remember, however, that their vitamin content diminishes progressively in relation to the length of time they are out of the ground. Growing potatoes in my own garden, I find it very rewarding to cook them straight from the soil, when they are still perfect with smooth pale skins free of blemishes.

They are the most adaptable of vegetables; they can be baked, boiled, steamed or fried. Grated, they may be made into pancakes from the Jewish *latkes* to the Swiss *rösti*; they can be mashed and mixed with flour to make gnocchi, scones, little cakes or even bread. Pureed, they can form the base for a soufflé, or made into a sweet cake with apples. Mashed, they can be used as a covering for a savory pie. They make a good creamy soup in combination with leeks or onions, and parsley. They can even be used as a garnish: one plain boiled potato in a bowl of steaming hot borsch is an exquisite and appetizing sight.

When I was living in Paris just after leaving school, my first choice on being taken to a restaurant was a broiled pork chop on a potato puree, and nothing has ever tasted better; I have been repeating it ever since. I make the puree by pushing boiled potatoes through a strainer and then putting them in a clean pan in a warm place to dry out while in another pan I heat a generous amount of butter with some milk, adding plenty of sea salt and freshly ground black pepper; this I beat into the potatoes until all is light and almost liquid. If it is not to be served at once, I pour a film of melted butter and hot milk over the surface to prevent a skin forming, keep it hot in the oven and beat the surface liquid in at the last moment. To me this is the best of all accompaniments for broiled or roasted meat, poultry or fish. Leftover mashed potatoes need never be wasted. Mixed with chopped cabbage or kale, they become "bubble and squeak." A flat cake of mashed potato mixed with fried onion and browned in a frying pan makes a splendid accompaniment to bacon and eggs for supper.

As a schoolgirl in the north of Scotland I sometimes spent Saturdays with other children in the fields gathering potatoes. We were paid a shilling an hour. It was grueling work, involving continual stooping for six or seven hours. In the evening, when it had grown too dark to see the potatoes clearly, we used to make a bonfire and roast some of the day's harvest in the ashes, before riding home on the tractor. The smell of roasting potatoes always brings back the exhilarating feeling of relief at having managed to get through the long day, for the other children were much tougher than I was.

Those Scottish potatoes were good, but not as delicious as those I was to eat later in Ireland, where they almost always attain what I can only call perfection: boiled in their skins, drained and left to steam under a folded cloth for a few minutes, then dished up and sent to the table, with their brown skins splitting here and there and the floury white flesh bursting through.

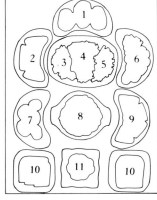

1 *Baked potatoes*
2 *Rösti*
3 *French-fried potatoes*
4 *Waffle-cut potatoes*
5 *Shoestring potatoes*
6 *Potato gnocchi*
7 *Pot-roasted potatoes*
8 *Potato dauphinois*
9 *Potato scones*
10 *Potato bread*
11 *Pommes Anna*

Pasta galore

Delicious, so easy to cook and supremely versatile, pasta comes in all shapes and sizes and can be simply glistened with oil or dressed up for dinner with an exotic sauce

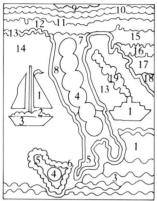

1 Lasagne
2 Tomato paste
3 Lasagne verdi
4 Capelli d'angelo
5 Rotelle
6 Anelli
7 Gramigna
8 Ditalini
9 Pagliaccio
10 Tortellini
11 Riccioli
12 Farfalle
13 Chifferi
14 Linguine
15 Margherite
16 Rigatoni
17 Stelline
18 Conchigliette
19 Taglierini verdi

Pasta takes myriad forms: stars, shells, wheels, letters of the alphabet, strips or tubes of various colors and countless different thicknesses and lengths. Admittedly most are made from the same basic mixture, but a new look can be given to a dish by using one of the less usual shapes.

There are three main varieties of pasta: first, the majority, like spaghetti, made from white semolina flour; second, the same paste enriched with eggs, usually for noodles; third, the basic paste colored green by the addition of spinach, made into lasagne and noodles of varying sizes.

Spaghetti is probably most people's idea of a cheap and easy meal, and it is indeed one of the most convenient and inexpensive of foods. Easy to cook, capable of being stored for reasonable periods of time, it is popular with almost everyone, including children and vegetarians, when covered with one or another of a wide variety of sauces.

When eating in certain Italian restaurants in London I am likely to be seduced by the sight of that day's freshly made pasta—usually noodles in green and white—lying in soft nests on the cart alongside the hors d'oeuvre. These are a far cry from the dried pasta we buy in packets from the grocer. In Soho one can buy green and white noodles, freshly made each day, or choose from a vast selection of pasta shapes kept in separate windowed drawers of huge chests.

Pale brown pasta made from whole wheat or buckwheat flour is something I cannot recommend too highly, especially a very thin buckwheat spaghetti, which I serve with a sauce of thinly sliced vegetables—leeks, carrots, and onions—gently stewed in oil and eaten in the Japanese manner, while still slightly crisp, with soy sauce or sesame salt added. I would not serve it with a very meaty sauce—the nutty buckwheat flavor has a special affinity with vegetables; but with a carbonara sauce it is a revelation.

Whole wheat spaghettis and macaronis are also acceptable although less delicate in flavor. A whole wheat macaroni is good in minestrone; the pale brown color merges nicely with the other ingredients, and the taste and slightly firmer texture go well with them too. When I was in Vermont recently, a friend recommended a spaghetti made from Jerusalem artichokes. It was quite delicious, and I am disappointed not to have found its equivalent in England.

As a main dish, I usually serve spaghettini or noodles with one or another vegetable mixture, or a sauce of clams, mussels or other shellfish, or a nut sauce. I rarely make meat sauces, but I like a chicken and vegetable sauce very much.

The other shapes of pasta I am apt to prefer without a sauce, simply dressed with butter or oil and served as an accompaniment to another dish—a meat stew, for instance. Seafood sauces can be delicious but are rarely seen in England; a quick last-minute dish can be made from canned minced clams, which are very good. An uncooked sauce can be made by combining in a blender canned Italian tomatoes, some chopped salami, flaked tuna fish and chopped black olives, with a little oregano; blend well, and pour, cold, over hot spaghetti. In summer, spaghetti can also be eaten cold. In this case it must be well moistened with plenty of olive oil or dressed with a suitably oily sauce; it can be tossed from time to time while cooling.

44

The goodness of grains

Grains in their less well-known varieties are staple foods in many countries, but their excitingly different flavors are too often overlooked by unadventurous cooks

Although grains are among the world's leading staple foods, they have been sadly neglected in England. The only large-scale use the English have made of grain is wheat in its most refined form, as the basis of white bread and flour. In Scotland, on the other hand, oatmeal has been a basic source of nourishment since time immemorial, in soups (such as cullen skink), in haggis and porridge and delicious oatcakes. As potatoes have proved themselves an unreliable crop, it would seem sensible for us to explore other possibilities of basic nourishment. Rice and spaghetti have been adopted into our national cuisine, but beyond that none but the "health food freaks" have ventured. I find this sad, for we have chosen to ignore a rich and interesting family of foods, as anyone who has traveled in Eastern Europe and the Middle East will know.

Perhaps because I grew up in Scotland, where we ate porridge every day, I have a deep affection for these sustaining and nourishing foods, and look immediately for the foreign equivalents whenever I travel.

At the top of my list is *kasha*, the buckwheat that was the staple food of the Russian peasants, while in a more refined form it was made into the blinis of the rich. The whole buckwheat groats can be purchased roasted or plain. The roasted variety is better but more expensive; one can achieve the same result by stirring the unroasted buckwheat carefully in a heavy pan over low heat for four or five minutes, then leaving it to cool before cooking. I like to cook a quantity of buckwheat and keep it in the refrigerator, to be reheated with groups of fried vegetables as needed. It is good with just fried onions, but it needs some addition of this sort. A bowl of sesame salt should accompany it to the table. This can be bought, or can be made at home by pounding seven parts of sesame seeds with one part salt; this should be kept tightly bottled as it tends to lose its flavor.

Another of my favorites is cracked wheat, known as *bulgur* in Turkey and *burghul* in the Middle East. It is extremely nourishing, in either hot or cold dishes, and is inexpensive.

Couscous is the staple food of Morocco, which as a result of the French occupation became very popular in France, after the French refined and vastly improved what was originally a rough peasant food. In Paris there are many restaurants on the Left Bank which devote themselves entirely to different dishes of couscous.

The first time I ate couscous, in a small restaurant built up against the walls of Taroudant, in central Morocco, I found it perfectly disgusting. It was only years later, after eating it in a restaurant in the Rue des Saint-Pères in Paris, that I became aware of its delicious possibilities.

White polished rice is less nutritious than unpolished brown rice, which can be made into tasty dishes, yet I continue to use white rice to accompany meat dishes, because the brown variety adds a heavy quality that is not always desirable. Wild rice is aptly named in relation to its price. It is a real luxury and part of its appeal lies in its rarity; thus it is delicious eaten occasionally in small quantities. It does make a splendid stuffing for quail or other game birds.

Wheat germ is a versatile and delicious food. An unsweetened form, rather like bran, can be sprinkled on salads and vegetable dishes. A crunchy, sweetened variety, which is perfectly delicious and not really sweet in taste, is considered best of all in my house. We eat it in plain yogurt as a dessert. I find it also makes a good and unusual ice cream, along the lines of an old-fashioned English brown bread ice.

In the range of grains, an Italian import worth a mention is *polenta*, which I like occasionally as an accompaniment to game. Or it can be made into little cakes and fried; in this way it is served with cocktails at Harry's Bar in Venice.

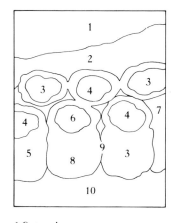

1 *Oatmeal*
2 *Brown rice*
3 *Millet*
4 *Wheat germ*
5 *Polenta*
6 *Buckwheat*
7 *Semolina*
8 *Pourgouri (Cypriot cracked wheat)*
9 *Cracked wheat*
10 *Wild rice*

buckwheat kasha with
  egg p110
cracked wheat risotto p110
cracked wheat salad p110
couscous with
  vegetables p110
rice and yogurt salad p111
vegetables with brown
  rice p111
polenta p111
wheatgerm ice cream p118

The delights of bread-making

Soft chapatis, Irish soda bread, saffron loaves and Russian pirog – just a sampling of the many delicious varieties of the simplest and most satisfying of foods

1 *Finnish rye bread with green cabbage filling*

2 *Saffron bread*

3 *Onion bread*

4 *Russian pirog with mushroom filling*

5 *Onion rolls*

Making bread has always seemed to me one of the most creative forms of cookery, whereby, with the addition of water and yeast, plain flour is transformed into a hot and fragrant loaf. It is at the same time the simplest and the most mysterious of processes. Anyone who has worked with live yeast will know the strange feeling of handling the growing organism; watching it double in volume continues to amaze me.

Like all really pure and basic processes, it is virtually impossible to spoil. I don't think I have ever seen a loaf of bread that was not visually pleasing, for decoration beyond a certain degree is not really practical. Those who enjoy decorating their food at length will prefer cake-making—something that has never attracted me.

One of the most appealing aspects of bread is its history, for it is one of the most ancient of foods, and has changed little over the centuries. It is rich in symbolism, and figures in religious ceremonies and traditional rules of friendship and hospitality in many different cultures. There are few countries where bread does not form part of the staple diet. It is often the poorest countries that have the most delicious and interesting breads. Irish soda bread, for example, or the breads of India: the soft *chapati* which takes the place of rice in northern India, and is used as a vehicle for the spicy dishes of that region, and the delicious *nan*, cooked in a matter of moments in the fierce tandoori ovens, stuck against the walls of the oven like pieces of chewing gum. In parts of China they make a steamed bread which I have always longed to try, while in the Middle Eastern countries they make a flat bread, round or oval in shape, with a hollow pouch in the middle. This *pita* bread can be bought at Middle Eastern, Greek or Cypriot food shops.

I have tried to make it many times, but with no success. I even had a friend bring me back a bag of flour from the Lebanon, with instructions from a local baker, but to no avail.

It is a strange anomaly that such an ancient food should respond so well to modern technological developments, for not only does bread freeze remarkably well—it can be frozen either before baking, or even halfway through the rising—but the refrigerator can also be used to slow down the actual rising process.

Bread-making is a simple but lengthy process; it is not particularly economical, for the cost of good flour is almost the same as that of bread. But it is very rewarding. I would suggest, however, that if you are going to the trouble of making your own bread you try something more unusual than the ordinary loaf, after mastering the basics. Saffron bread, for instance, adapted from an early English recipe, makes an especially good accompaniment to a *soupe au pistou*, a fish soup, or a ratatouille. It is also good toasted, or made into croutons to serve with bouillabaisse. Onion bread is also delicious, and can turn an ordinary *pâté de campagne* into a memorable meal; it is good too with fish pâtés, or vegetable hors d'oeuvre. The Russian *pirog* is fairly tricky to make, and not recommended for a first attempt at bread-making. It is similar to a brioche dough, and the high fat content makes it sticky to handle. It is extremely good, however, and makes a substantial and delicious meatless meal when served with two or three hot vegetable dishes. The Finnish rye bread can be made with a vegetable filling, but it is also good unfilled; it is a firm dark bread with a good flavor. I also include a recipe for a plain white loaf; for anyone who has not made bread before, this is good to start with.

48

$\mathcal{A}$ hoard of nuts

*Among the most nutritious of foods, nuts are a highly concentrated source of energy —
and, in some unexpected ways, the source of fine flavors in many exciting dishes*

The gathering of nuts has been a part of the English rural scene for hundreds of years but, strangely, cooking with nuts is rare. While nuts and raisins are sometimes eaten at the end of a meal, apart from the stuffing for the Christmas turkey, nuts figure little in contemporary English cookery. Even in baking, there is only the occasional walnut cake, or macaroon. In France, on the other hand, there are many delicious cakes and pastries based on nuts. When I lived in Paris as a young girl, one of my favorites was a sort of biscuit made of a meringue mixture of hazel nuts and egg whites, sandwiched together with a coffee-flavored cream. In the United States, pecans, walnuts, almonds and peanuts are sometimes added to cake mixtures, or scattered whole over ice cream sundaes or banana splits, and pecan pie is a favorite dish of the southern states, but these are little known in England.

Since my own sweet tooth is very nearly nonexistent, I prefer the way nuts are used in Middle Eastern countries. In Syria and Lebanon, pine nuts are scattered over rice dishes or mixed with stuffings for green peppers. In Turkey, walnuts are combined with bread crumbs in a delicate sauce for chicken; ground almonds are used as a thickening for sauces in Egypt, and walnuts often complement the local sour plums in dishes in the Armenian/Georgian region of Russia. Farther east, in Burma and Malaysia, peanuts are ground into delicious oily sauces for serving with *satay*, tiny skewers of grilled meat. In parts of central Africa peanuts are blended with vegetables to make soups and sauces.

Nuts are among the most nutritious of foods, and have been used in many cultures as a substitute for meat, since they contain many of the same properties. Almonds and Brazil nuts are particularly rich in iron and calcium, while peanuts are a valuable source of protein and phosphorus. All nuts are a highly concentrated source of energy; a handful of nuts and raisins is a quick and sustaining snack. Unfortunately, all nuts are very high in fat content, so they are not really suitable for those on diets.

One of my favorites is the pine nut. This is the kernel of a special pine tree found in Lebanon, Greece and Italy. The only nut widely grown in England is the so-called "Kentish cob," really a filbert. These are delicious eaten fresh in the autumn, and so are green walnuts before they have been dried.

A fairly recent development in nuts came with the discovery of the macadamia nut in Australia at the end of the nineteenth century, by a Dr Macadam. These trees have since been introduced into Hawaii, where they are now widely grown, and a few other places including Malawi. Macadamia nuts have such hard shells that they cannot be cracked by hand, and must be shelled by machinery, which makes them very expensive. They are packed and sold in glass jars and in cans. They do not have the oily quality of most nuts, and have an unusual subtle taste. They are good with cocktails, chopped in salads, or scattered over sweet dishes.

In medieval times, nuts were much more evident in English cookery than today. "Almond milk," used both as a thickening agent and as a flavoring, appears again and again in recipes from the fourteenth century onward, particularly for soups, dishes of fish or chicken and sweet dishes. It was included as an ingredient in a dish of lobsters and rice served at Henry IV's coronation feast. It was also found in early versions of cold dishes of chicken, aspics of calves' feet and meat loaves; and a recipe for salmon and eels called for cooking them in a combination of almond milk and verjuice, a slightly fermented crabapple juice also much in use in early English cookery. (This last dish illustrates an early form of sweet/sour cooking.) During the seventeenth and eighteenth centuries, the use of almond milk declined. Its place was probably taken by the use of spices, whose popularity spread with the growth of trade with the East. In the nineteenth century, an essence of bitter almonds called *ratafia* was used in making cakes and biscuits, but by that time the use of nuts in all forms was sadly declining as the bland preferences of Queen Victoria and her household began their depressing effect on our national cuisine.

1 Cob nuts (filberts)
2 Hazelnuts

A touch of spice

Evoke faraway places with the fragrant aromas of spices. Pungent or subtle, they give even the very simplest of food an interesting touch of individuality

1 *Paprika, mustard powder, cumin, cardamom seeds, mixed spices*
2 *Cloves*
3 *Black mustard seed, sea salt*
4 *Ground fenugreek, whole fenugreek, dried red pepper*
5 *Dried marigold petals*
6 *Mustard powder, whole fenugreek, dried yellow pepper*
7 *Dried rosebuds*
8 *Mixed pickling spices*
9 *Turmeric*
10 *Grey poppy seeds*
11 *Peppercorns*
12 *White poppy seeds, juniper berries, star anise*
13 *Sesame seeds, star anise*
14 *Cristalo, juniper berries, star anise*
15 *Mustard seed*
16 *Juniper berries, red chili peppers*
17 *Lemon grass*
18 *Licorice root*
19 *Mustard powder*
20 *Red chili peppers*
21 *Cinnamon sticks*

Spices are among the most aromatically evocative of all ingredients. Their mere smell calls to mind foreign places and each combination of spices has its own special character. A mixture of cumin and coriander, for instance, evokes memories of India and the Middle East for me, while, with the addition of cinnamon and chili a Moroccan flavor instantly emerges.

Spices have become as important to me in winter as fresh herbs are in summer. They fill similar roles, enlivening basically simple food and adding an individual touch to one's cooking. Many of our winter foods are bland and lend themselves to the addition of certain spices. One thing I like to have on hand is the French blend known as *quatre épices*; but one can duplicate this easily enough by adding one pinch each of nutmeg, cloves and cinnamon to one teaspoon of finely ground black pepper.

After years of making unsatisfactory curries using prepared curry powder, I ventured out and bought a selection of relevant spices in an Indian spice shop. Since then I have always stuck to my own mixtures. I make only mild curries of fish, chicken, vegetables or eggs, although I love to eat fiery lamb *dhansak* in an Indian restaurant. After experimenting with different proportions, I settled on a rough formula of equal parts ground cumin, coriander and turmeric with a half part of ground chili pepper. For dishes other than curries, too, coriander and cumin are useful. I use them interchangeably or mixed in equal parts, particularly in dishes of cabbage, mushrooms or zucchini. One teaspoon each of ground coriander, ground cumin and celery salt makes a delicious seasoning for hard-boiled eggs.

Turmeric gives a warm spicy taste to rice, onions or fish, and ground juniper berries are incredibly good with sauerkraut and all cabbage dishes, and pork or game. Allspice is very subtle, tasting curiously like a blend of cloves, nutmeg and cinnamon, although it is in fact the ground berry of one tree. It can be used alone for sweet dishes, or combined with generous amounts of black pepper for savory ones. My favorite spice of all is saffron, and this is too special and too expensive to mix with any other. I once ate a risotto in a restaurant in Vicenza at two in the morning, after attending *Manon Lescaut* in the open-air opera house; the risotto consisted of nothing more extraordinary than rice, onions, butter, chicken stock and saffron, but it was one of the best dishes I have ever eaten.

Although the use of spices is ancient, there has been a new development in the past few years, in the harvesting of peppercorns. First the soft green peppercorn appeared, and this has since been followed by the dried green peppercorn; now there is a pink peppercorn bottled in vinegar. The soft green peppercorns are available in cans from specialty food shops. I add a whole can of them to duck pâté; they add a marvelous sharp juicy taste to the usual "hot" pepper flavor.

The delicate spices we use in sweet dishes—cinnamon, vanilla, ginger and nutmeg—are no less delicious than the more robust spices. The genuine vanilla pod gives off its subtle flavor which delights me each time I make a *sauce à la vanille*, or any of the exquisite puddings based on it, such as floating island (*oeufs en neige*). Apple desserts, such as apple Charlotte and apple crumble, benefit from the addition of cinnamon. Another good dessert is a delicious spiced fruit bread which I learned to make as they do in Cumberland. I enjoy making it, and I like it better than any cake I know.

Fresh flavors from dried fruit

Bring a taste of sunshine to warming winter dishes with the goodness that is stored in dried apricots, figs and apples, pears, grapes, peaches and plums

Drying has a curious effect on fruit; it alters its character completely, turning it into something quite different. Who could guess that a raisin was once a grape, or a prune originally a plum? Not only does the process of dehydration change the consistency, flavor and color of the fruit, it intensifies certain properties: both dried apricots and prunes are higher in food value than in their original state, and raisins are more nutritious than grapes. The calorie count also increases, though.

Hundreds of years ago, dried fruits were enormously popular in England. In the thirteenth century they were imported from Portugal and the Levant, and by Elizabethan times every household of any size had a larder well stocked with dried figs, dates and raisins. In that period, dishes of mixed sweet and savory foods were very much in vogue in England, as they have continued to be in some Middle Eastern countries. In a fifteenth-century English cookbook we find capon with dried figs, and huge pies combining beef, game and poultry, beef marrow and suet, with prunes, dates and raisins, saffron, mace and cinnamon. In a seventeenth-century book are the instructions for cooking salt cod, hard-boiled eggs, spinach and parsley with raisins and currants, and candied orange and lemon peel.

Further, these intricate English dishes are amazingly like many to be found in a thirteenth-century Persian manuscript: here are numerous descriptions of dishes combining meat or chicken with dried apricots, quinces, prunes, apples and currants—similar to certain dishes found in North Africa today. In these, also, the combining of such diverse ingredients is helped by the addition of saffron, spices and nuts.

In the twentieth century, dried fruit has sadly enjoyed little popularity in England, at least until the advent of health food shops. (Too many of us were put off prunes at school.) In the United States, prune juice is popular and prunes are often eaten stewed for breakfast.

The large California prunes are also good eaten raw, and can be made into elegant desserts—soufflés, mousses and whips. These can be both delicious and pretty, for the subtle color of the prune contrasts admirably with the whipped cream which so often accompanies it. Some dehydrated fruits are so lightly dried that they do not need soaking; indeed, they are often plump and soft enough to eat straight from the packet. My favorite is dried peaches, which I cook very lightly so that they are only just soft and still quite chewy. They are delicious served still warm, with lightly whipped cream mixed with yogurt. Dried pears are also extremely good, and apple rings, apricots, figs and raisins can be used in countless different ways.

Mixed dried fruit makes a good winter fruit salad, with whipped cream and chopped nuts. A mixture of dried fruits, cut in tiny pieces and fried in butter with a chopped onion, makes an unusual stuffing for a roast chicken, duck or game bird. For adventurous cooks, there are many interesting dishes of stewed lamb, veal or chicken with dried fruits used in making the sauce. The inevitable sweetness that results from the addition of the fruit can be counteracted by adding a little lemon juice at the last minute.

A very good paste made from dried apricots can be bought in shops that specialize in Eastern delicacies; it is called (phonetically) *Kamar-el-deen*. The paste dissolves when soaked overnight in water. It needs no cooking and can be made immediately into mousses, ice cream or whips, and it makes a delicious drink when put in the blender (after soaking) with buttermilk or yogurt. It can also be eaten straight from the packet, as a sort of chewy sweet.

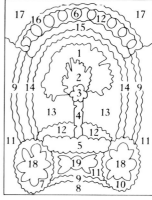

1 *Citron; dried apricots*
2 *Angelica*
3 *Glacéed cherries*
4 *Dried bananas*
5 *Figs*
6 *Dried peaches*
7 *Currants*
8 *Sultanas*
9 *Prunes*
10 *Raisins*
11 *Dried apple*
12 *Chopped mixed peel*
13 *Dried coconut*
14 *Dates*
15 *Dried pear; apricots*
16 *Prunes; dried apricots*
17 *Kamar-el-deen*
18 *Dried pears, peaches; candied pineapple, orange peel*
19 *Dried peaches; candied pineapple, orange peel*

chicken stuffed with dried fruit p81
veal with apricots p90
Moroccan lamb with pears p91
dried-fruit salad p115
prune mousse p116

Exotic fruits

Sadly neglected in their fresh form in all but their homelands, tropical fruits are fragrant and irresistible in their mouthwatering shades of pink, orange and green

1 *Sugar cane*
2 *Lychee nuts*
3 *Kumquats*
4 *Papaya*
5 *Mango*
6 *Green Jamaican orange*
7 *Pomegranate*
8 *Passion fruit*
9 *Chinese gooseberry (Kiwi fruit)*

Tropical fruits have an exotic appeal, both visual and symbolic, that acts strongly on those of us who live in temperate countries, especially during the gloomy midwinter months. These strange and intriguing fruits come as a welcome contrast to our own more familiar varieties. Yet apart from the pineapple and the avocado (which we treat as a vegetable) these fruits have not been widely adopted by northern peoples. The British are happy to eat canned lychees or mango in the form of chutney in Chinese or Indian restaurants, but we seem wary of buying the fruits in their fresh state.

Almost their strongest appeal is that of sight and smell, for these fruits are almost without exception in mouthwatering shades of pink, orange and green, often in contrast to their exterior skins; most of them have a strong fragrance. To be honest, I often find their taste something of a disappointment; they nearly all share a curious bland texture not unlike that of the avocado, and a sweet rich flavor. Others are so richly endowed with seeds as to be almost unmanageable, like the passion fruit. Yet their special qualities should not be overlooked, for they can be made into ravishingly pretty dishes, ideal for serving in small quantities to end a dinner party.

The mango, which has a strange heavy taste, is a curiously difficult fruit to eat. It must first be peeled, and then the flesh needs to be cut from the seed even when the mango is ripe, which can result in much messy pulp and juice. It is the best-loved fruit of India, where some two million acres are devoted to growing mangoes, of which about five million tons a year are produced. They can be made into dessert dishes, but I prefer them cooked when still green, to make the best of all chutneys. More delicious I think is the papaya. This can be mixed with other fruits, but is best, in my opinion, simply peeled and cut in cubes, sprinkled generously with lime juice, and chilled for two or three hours before eating.

The guava is a strange fruit, rich in vitamin C, very sweet, and with a strong aroma. It can be included in a mixture of tropical fruits, but I like it best made into guava jelly, which is so delicious when eaten with cream cheese. Passion fruit, usually with a funny wrinkled skin, has a more appealing fresh tart flavor, but its

disadvantage is the multitude of tiny seeds; these are almost impossible to separate from the flesh. I do not mind them just as I do not mind the seeds in raspberry jam, but for others more fussy than I am the only answer is to put them through a sieve. This will give you only a small amount of pulpy juice; but it is good for adding to a fruit salad or sorbet.

Chinese gooseberries (or Kiwi fruit as they are called in New Zealand) are, on the other hand, simplicity itself to eat, and are extremely pretty when cut in slices, with a few black seeds nestling in the pale green flesh. They can be sliced and added to salads, eaten with yogurt, or simply cut in half and eaten with a teaspoon. I like to use them in a dish of mixed pale green and yellow fruit, with honeydew melon, pineapple and lime juice.

Almost prettiest of all the exotic fruits is the lychee, little known in America except in the dried form called lychee nut. When fresh, its hard red shell opens to reveal a pearly-white fruit shaped like a small bird's egg with a luscious sheen. In mixed fruit salads these are excellent, or simply served alone, in a thin syrup flavored tartly with fresh lime juice. Many of these unusual fruits make exquisite sorbets, rather than ice cream, for they are too rich for mixing with cream and egg yolks. Alternatively they can be cut in small pieces and served with scoops of tart sorbets made from other fruits such as raspberry, lemon or lime.

Pomegranates are an exceptionally sweet fruit, but the original wild pomegranate, like the Seville orange, was bitter; years of cross-breeding have resulted in the familiar sweet pomegranate which is the only one we find in our shops. I like to use them simply as decoration, for it is a remarkably pretty fruit and one that can be kept for weeks without losing any of its beauty; the dark pink skin simply hardens slightly into a shell-like exterior. I encountered the bitter pomegranate for the first time recently in Spain; it is sad they are not available elsewhere for they give one of the best fruit juices I have ever tasted, which is a beautiful dark crimson in color. The juice of the sweet pomegranate is used commercially to make grenadine syrup, which is much loved in France. Some like it poured over ice cream, but I much prefer it in cocktails.

Old-fashioned puddings

Forget the fashion for fresh fruit and yogurt and finish off a light meal with a hearty English pudding sticky with syrup and jam or adorned with fruit

Some of the best-loved dishes in England, especially popular with foreign visitors and with the English themselves, are our hot puddings. (The word "pudding" is used by the English to refer to the sweet course, whether a true pudding or not.) The dishes I have in mind are indeed true puddings, in that they are composed of flour, butter and eggs, with various additions. These are the same basic ingredients that go into the making of a cake, but the pudding mixture is usually moister, and is often steamed rather than being baked.

Many of the best old English puddings have been forgotten, though a few still remain popular. While rice pudding, bread and butter pudding, and jam pancakes can still be found on the menus of some old-fashioned hotels and restaurants, others are practically never seen except occasionally in private houses. This may be due in part to the modern avoidance of fattening food, and to the fact that many of us have taken to ending our meals with fruit and cheese, or yogurt. But in midwinter, when yogurt seems a trifle chilly, a hot pudding can make the perfect end to a light meal; there is something very heartening about it, particularly on weekends and holidays. Some puddings take time to make, but with the help of modern machines for mixing sponge and making bread crumbs, this may not be a problem.

Among my favorites as a child were "castle puddings," which reminded me of sand castles, in the shape of tiny inverted buckets. These were always served, like many other puddings of this sort, with a delicious sauce made from syrup heated with a little lemon juice.

England is the only country I know that grows apples expressly for cooking, so of course there is a wide range of apple puddings—these apples combine so well with the bland tastes of sponge, bread and cream. "Eve's pudding" is one of the best: simply a dish half-filled with stewed apples

under a topping of soft sponge, served hot with cream. Almost every pudding I can think of is improved by cream, except for those which contain citrus fruits.

Some of the hot jam puddings are also very good: "queen of puddings" in particular, with layers of soft bread crumbs, jam and meringue. Treacle tart is almost too sweet for me, though many people love it. There is another very popular toffee pudding made with fingers of bread soaked first in milk and then in a hot toffee sauce. Many of the best puddings are based on bread; the mixture of crisply fried bread with juicy apples is one of the best imaginable.

Most widely known of all English puddings is of course the plum pudding, or Christmas pudding. There must be literally thousands of different recipes, and they vary hugely. The one I like best is a comparatively light mixture, with brandy and a lot of fruit but neither flour nor sugar; it is not quite so rich and dark as some, but is more to my taste. It recalls one often served in Scotland when I was a child, although that version had less fruit and no brandy. It was called "seven cup pudding," and was simplicity itself to make. Although very similar to a plum pudding, it was made and eaten on the same day. I cannot help feeling that the inordinately lengthy steaming, in two sessions, that is traditional for English Christmas puddings, is not really essential, as our one-day version, although lighter in color than the other, was always delicious.

I wish I enjoyed Christmas pudding more on the actual day. I feel sure that it is because it follows the turkey with its rich stuffing that I invariably feel so uncomfortably full afterwards. I think one year I shall change the plan and serve both dishes, but at separate meals: perhaps have the turkey at midday with a light citrus fruit salad to counteract the heaviness of the stuffing, and in the evening serve baked ham and a salad, followed by the pudding in all its glory.

1 *Brandy butter*
2 *Buttered apples*
3 *Golden syrup sauce*
4 *Grapes and peaches*
5 *Rice pudding*
6 *Christmas pudding*
7 *Queen of puddings*
8 *Castle puddings*
9 *Jam tarts*
10 *Turkish delight and*
    sugared almonds
11 *Mince pies*

The essence of coffee

The history of coffee is as colorful as its popularity is constant. It has a strong, almost compulsive appeal, both as a drink and as a flavoring in ice creams and other desserts

1 *Black coffee*
2 *Macaroon*
3 *Amaretti*
4 *Candied melon*
5 *Figs*
6 *Chocolates*
7 *Glacéed fruit*
8 *Crystallized fruits; fondants*
9 *Cherries in brandy*
10 *Chocolate mints*
11 *Nuts; dates*
12 *Nuts*
13 *Grapes*
14 *Pineapple*
15 *Oranges*

When the price of coffee rises sharply, I, like other coffee addicts, find myself unable either to find a substitute or to go without. In fact, the realization that I am actually prepared to pay inflated prices makes me appreciate it more.

Apart from the joys of coffee drinking, I have long been fond of it as a flavoring for sweet dishes, for ice creams, mousses and custards. I find it delicious combined with chocolate, with nuts and with cream. When used as a flavoring, only very small amounts are needed, so the price becomes of less importance. There is an Italian instant coffee available in individual foil packets which I find extremely useful for making small quantities, and when wanted it can also be made double or triple strength.

The history of the coffee bean makes a fascinating story. The plant, *Caffea arabica*, originated in Abyssinia, where it still grows wild. It was discovered by Arabs, who took it back with them to Aden and the Yemen where there are records of coffee drinking as early as the ninth century. Its anti-soporific properties made it much prized by devout Moslems, who used it to keep awake during long nocturnal prayers. It was not known in Western Europe until the mid-seventeenth century, when it was brought back from the East by travelers for their own use. It reached Venice in 1615, Marseilles in 1644, and Paris in 1647. It did not become generally known in France until 1669, when the Turkish ambassador started serving it to his guests, as he was accustomed to do at home. It quickly became the fashion in Paris.

The first coffee house in London was opened in 1652 by an Englishman called Edwards. He had recently returned from Smyrna (where he had been British Consul) bringing a native servant with him. Encouraged by his friends' enthusiasm, he set up his servant in a small coffee house, and it succeeded at once. Soon coffee houses were springing up like mushrooms, becoming the accepted places for seeing one's friends and hearing the latest news; by the early eighteenth century there were nearly 500 such meeting places in London.

The coffee bean reached Vienna in a most romantic way. When the Turks were defeated in their third attempt at conquering the city in 1683, they were forced to withdraw, leaving behind a vast encampment of more than 500,000 tents with all their provisions. These included sacks of coffee beans, at first thought to be food for camels. However the hungry Viennese soon realized their mistake, and learned for the first time to roast and brew coffee. They strained it, which the Turks and Arabs never did, and drank it mixed with milk and honey.

The love of coffee houses spread quickly among the Viennese, and has never left them. They have a gift for making coffee houses welcoming and comfortable, like a home away from home, with newspapers and magazines, chess and checkers. Vienna is still full of these delightful places, where as many as 27 different sorts of coffee are sometimes served, as well as hot chocolate, ices, cakes and pastries. There is a charming custom among the Viennese of having a meal in a restaurant or beer parlor, then moving to a coffee house for dessert and coffee.

The worldwide spread of coffee was greatly influenced by the East Indian coffee trade, started by the Dutch in 1690, when they began to grow coffee in Java.

In the reign of Louis XIV, the French introduced the plant to Martinique, where it flourished, and later to French Guiana, from where it spread to Brazil and Central America. Two-thirds of the world's coffee now grows in Brazil, most of it exported to the United States. Opinions vary about the best quality, but general opinion seems to favor coffee grown in the Blue Mountains of Jamaica, and certain Central and South American countries such as Costa Rica and Colombia. Arabian coffee, particularly from the Yemen, is considered excellent, although unfortunately very little is exported.

Arabian or Turkish coffee, like that of the Greeks, is made in a totally different way from ours which makes it hard to compare the two. First, the beans are roasted dark, then ground powder fine. Both these operations are usually performed in the home, just before brewing. The ground coffee is then put with water and sugar in a small pot with a narrow neck and a long handle. Sometimes a few cardamom seeds are added. It is brought to the boil two or three times, with time to settle briefly in between. The ritual is central to Arab hospitality, and a guest will be served coffee as soon as possible after his arrival. The nature of the occasion may determine the degree of sugar to be added—after a wedding the coffee will be very sweet, while after a funeral it will invariably be bitter—but usually the guest will be asked how sweet he likes it, and it will be made accordingly.

The food of childhood

The yearning in adulthood for the simple dishes so beloved in childhood has led to a naïve but satisfying style of English cooking, a sort of "haute nursery"

As a concept, nursery food is peculiarly English; it just does not exist in any other language, and is virtually untranslatable. What it means, to me at any rate, is the sort of very simple English food which children used to eat in the nursery—such foods as sausages with mashed potato, Irish stew, liver and bacon, rice pudding and apple pie. Having eaten these things as small children, many Englishmen formed a lasting addiction to them. An Englishman of this type will be unimpressed by French or "gourmet" cooking and will continue to eat nursery food whenever he can get it, if not at home, then at his club, hotel, or favorite restaurant. At White's, one of the most distinguished of London's men's clubs, this need is understood, and there is hardly a day's menu without an acceptable dish of this sort. At Wilton's, one of the best and most expensive of all London's restaurants, liver and onions and sausages and mash are on the menu frequently, and what is more they are served by waitresses with a distinct aura of the nanny about them. Even the Connaught, filled as it is with foreign visitors, makes a point of offering one such dish beautifully cooked each day for their old-fashioned English clientele at lunchtime.

I cannot help feeling that this sort of food may soon cease to exist, for the next generation will have had no experience of the proper English nursery as it was, nor of its food. The modern child presumably eats the same food as his parents, and probably suffers from the passing trends, learning to adapt one day to ratatouille and to brown rice on another, without having any firm culinary background to return to in later years when feeling nostalgic.

In the prewar English house the nursery was a world of its own; it had its own timetable, hierarchy and diet. Since traditional English food is basically simple, it is ideally suited to the feeding of young children. Such dishes as Lancashire hotpot, fish pie, and Scotch broth (a thick soup of mutton, vegetables and barley) make ideal fare for children, and the vast range of English puddings, both hot and cold, seems tailor-made for the nursery.

It is not surprising that these dishes remain so popular with many Englishmen decades after they've outgrown the nursery. For it seems to me that it is in such dishes that the English have always excelled. The grander food of the sort that used to be served in old-fashioned English houses at dinner (after the children were in bed) is much less appealing. A sort of watered-down version of French cooking, it was likely to follow a monotonous pattern: a clear soup with some indiscriminate garnish floating in it, whitings served with their tails in their mouths, a meat dish often in a wine-based sauce, followed by a dessert or savory such as anchovies on toast. To me, certainly, as a small child growing up before the second world war, this sort of food fared poorly in comparison with the cozy sort of dishes we had in the nursery: creamy mashed potato with boiled beef and carrots, minced "collops" of beef served with little triangles of toast, macaroni and cheese, mushrooms on toast. There was little doubt in my mind who had the better deal.

One of my favorite cookbooks, Alexis Soyer's *The Modern Housewife*, published in 1856, recommends as a proper day's diet for children: "bread and milk for breakfast at eight; dinner at one, composed as follows through the week: roast mutton and apple pudding, roast beef and currant pudding, baked apples, boiled mutton with turnips, after which rice or vermicelli pudding; occasionally a little salt beef, with suet dumplings... or pease pudding... and at five o'clock, their bread and milk again, previous to going to bed." Bread and milk (which is the dish known in America as "milk toast") is something I never experienced. Perhaps it was never eaten in Scotland, or else it had gone out of fashion.

It must be admitted that when he returns to nursery food in later life, the choosy Englishman is served with slightly superior versions of his childhood favorites, a sort of "haute nursery." The Irish stew, for instance, would be made with the best cut of lamb trimmed into neat cutlets, and the cod in the fish pie would be replaced by a finer fish. But the dishes themselves, and their manner of cooking, remain unchanged.

1 Lancashire hotpot
2 Bread and butter pudding
3 Toad-in-the-hole
4 Cauliflower and cheese
5 Eggs
6 Boiled egg with brown bread and butter
7 Liver and bacon with onions and tomatoes
8 Milk

Christmas presents

Avoid the seasonal battle in the shops and conjure up Christmas gifts in the calm of your own kitchen. Pickles and pâtés, candies and jams are fun to make and delightful to receive

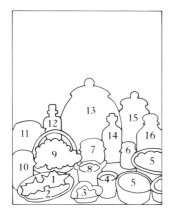

1 *Cinnamon cookies*
2 *Fudge*
3 *Coconut ice candies*
4 *Cumberland sauce*
5 *Pâté de campagne*
6 *Marmalade*
7 *Apricots in white wine*
8 *Rum butter*
9 *Frosted grapes*
10 *Preserved limes*
11 *Preserved lemons*
12 *Lemon vodka*
13 *Peaches in brandy*
14 *Cherries in brandy*
15 *Spiced melon*
16 *Sweet mustard pickle*

pâté de campagne p78
Cumberland sauce p105
apricots in white wine p116
spiced cookies p124
sloe gin p125
lemon vodka p125

I have always loved the idea of making things to eat for presents, and have in recent years actually put the idea into practice. Not only does it save time and money, it also avoids a rush in the shops.

For me, another reason to make gifts of food is that much as I enjoy making pickles and preserves, for some obscure reason once they are made I never actually want to open and eat them. A friend of mine, also a cookery writer, once confessed she could never bring herself to use the food she had made with such care for the freezer; perhaps we suffer the same neurosis. Presents I receive are different; I love being given things to eat and consume them immediately. Curiosity about other people's cooking makes it appeal to me more than my own. Eating one's own food inevitably brings a strong sense of déjà vu.

Bearing in mind the likelihood of cold turkey and ham in post-Christmas households, it is a good idea to make gifts of preserves that will complement this sort of cold food. The very English Cumberland sauce, for instance, is one of the nicest accompaniments to almost all cold meat. Spiced melon (or spiced melon rind) is delicous with cold ham, as is also a sweet mustard pickle. A good chutney would go well with curried turkey, but I have not yet succeeded in making one I like as much as the ones I can buy. A pâté makes a very acceptable present (particularly for someone living alone, as pâtés are not easily made on a small scale) and even better when accompanied by a small jar of Cumberland sauce, to be eaten with it. When made in pretty dishes and decorated with bay leaves and cranberries under a thin film of aspic, pâtés can be enchanting to look at. These should go into the refrigerator and be eaten within a week. If the pâté is sealed with a layer of melted lard, it will keep for several weeks in a cool place. In this case one puts the decoration into the bottom of the dish, before piling in the mixture. The pâté is then turned out before eating.

Rum or brandy butter keeps well, and makes a welcome present if the recipients have not already bought or made their own generous supply for the holidays. Another idea is home-made brandied mincemeat. A large glass jar of whole peaches in brandy (actually a brandy-flavored syrup) makes a handsome present; the

peaches keep for weeks, and can be eaten as a dessert or as accompaniment to baked ham. Dried apricots soaked in a sweet white wine, such as Sauternes, are easily made in small jars; prunes can be treated in the same way. Either of these goes well with after-dinner coffee. Spiced Christmas cookies made in seasonal shapes make good small presents, and can also be used to decorate the tree. Little packets of salted almonds are useful for last-minute presents; they should really be given, and eaten, the same day they are made. Homemade fudge and coconut ice candy wrapped in little bags of brightly colored cellophane and tied with ribbon make nice presents for visiting children. The frosted grapes in the picture are fun to prepare but are too fragile to wrap; they are best used as decorations for one's own Christmas table. Homemade drinks are splendid Christmas presents; sloe gin should have been made and bottled in October, but flavored vodkas can be made right up until the middle of December. My favorite is lemon vodka; hot chili peppers or fresh tarragon can also be used.

One shopping expedition will be necessary to buy the containers. For any foods that need vacuum sealing, I would suggest the French-type preserving jars with spring lids that can be used again and again. Small shallow earthenware dishes are the ideal containers for pâtés; they can usually be found in round or oval-shape brown glazed earthenware. Cookie cutters and small cake tins in pretty shapes—stars, hearts and fishes perhaps—will also be useful at this time.

Many preserves, which are good fun to make, will not need vacuum sealing due to their high content of vinegar, sugar or alcohol, but they will need to be kept in air-tight jars or the liquid will evaporate and the contents dry up. Rum and brandy butter can be packed into a jar without a lid, covered by a piece of greaseproof paper or foil, with a square of brightly patterned cotton fabric tied around the rim. A roll of colored cellophane and some ribbon is all that is needed for cookies, fudges and coconut ice candy, while aluminum foil and colored sticky tape will make an airtight wrapping for packets of salted almonds. Antique bottles, preferably in clear glass, are also worth keeping an eye out for, if you are planning to give any Christmas spirits.

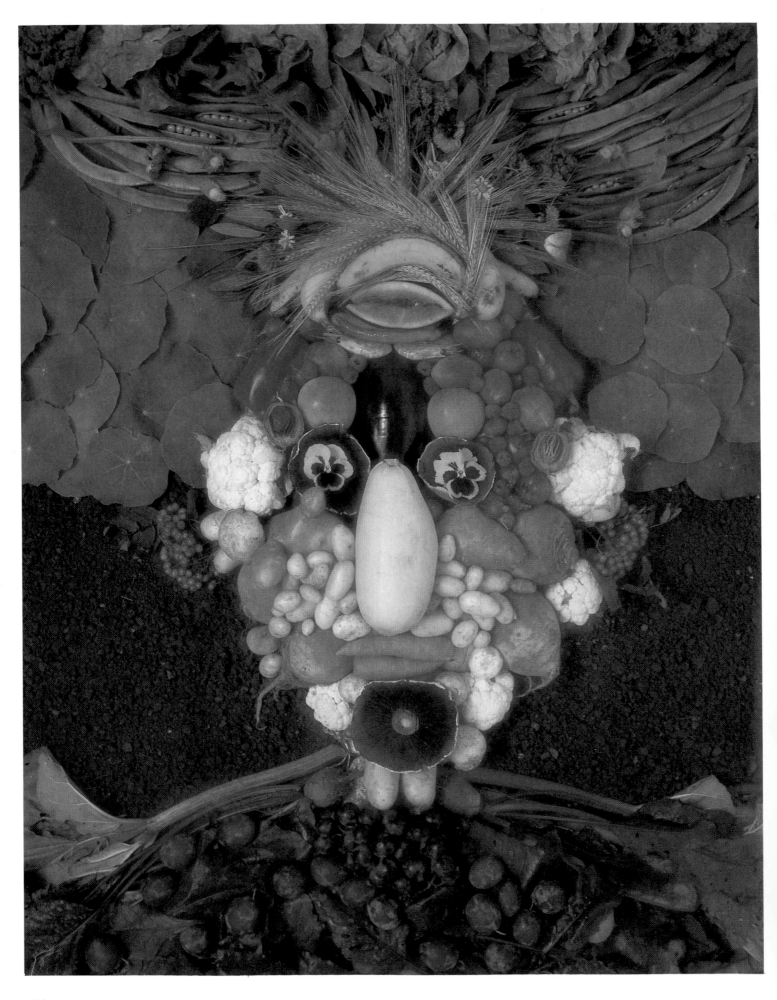

Winter recipes

The number of people each recipe serves is indicated wherever appropriate.

Soups/beans and vegetables

ribollita

This soup is traditionally made with the remains of yesterday's minestrone, the name ribollita meaning literally reboiled. I find it so good, however, that I make it for its own sake, even going so far as baking the bread

¼ lb dried cannellini beans (available in Italian food shops)

1 lb tomatoes

1 large onion

2 large carrots

3 stalks celery

1 head fennel

½ lb zucchini squash

4½ tablespoons olive oil

2 cloves garlic, crushed or minced

5 cups stock

6–8 thick slices bread (preferably homemade)

1 small head cabbage

salt and pepper

SERVES 6–8

The day before: put the beans into a pressure cooker, cover with cold water, and bring to the boil. Turn off the heat, cover the pan, and leave for one hour. Peel the tomatoes and cut in small pieces, discarding the seeds. Coarsely chop the onions, carrots, celery, fennel and zucchini. Heat 4 tablespoons of the oil in a heavy frying pan and cook all the vegetables gently for 8–10 minutes, stirring occasionally. Toward the end, add the garlic. Drain the beans, return them to the pressure cooker and add the vegetables with their juices. Add the stock to the cooker, cover, bring to the boil and cook under 15 pounds pressure for 20 minutes. Reduce the pressure until cover can be safely removed and test the beans. If they are still hard, cook under pressure for an additional 5 minutes. When they are soft, add salt and pepper to taste, and cool. Cover and refrigerate overnight. The next day, put the soup over low heat so that it reheats slowly. Meanwhile cook the cabbage, cut in quarters, in 2 cups of boiling salted water just until tender; drain and chop coarsely. Warm the soup bowls and lay a slice of bread in each one. Pile the cabbage on top of each piece of bread, ladle the hot soup over and sprinkle with olive oil.

Tuscan bean soup

¾ lb dried cannellini beans (available in Italian food shops)

3 tablespoons olive oil

2 cloves garlic

4 tablespoons chopped parsley

salt and pepper

SERVES 3–4

Soak the beans for 3–4 hours, or overnight. Drain, put in a pressure cooker and cover with 1¼ quarts cold water. Bring slowly to the boil, cover the pan and cook for 20 minutes under 15 pounds pressure. Reduce the pressure according to the manufacturer's directions, remove cover when safe and test the beans; if not yet soft, cook for another 5 minutes under pressure. (Alternatively, you can cook the beans without a pressure cooker: use a heavy pan and allow 1 hour's cooking time before testing the beans.) Add salt. Lift out about half of the beans with a slotted spoon, and reserve. Put the remaining beans with their cooking liquid into a blender and puree. Put the puree into a clean pan and add salt and pepper to taste. Stir in the whole beans. Heat gently, stirring often. Chop the garlic finely, and fry in the olive oil in a small frying pan. When lightly colored, add the parsley, then stir the mixture into the hot soup. Remove from the heat and stand, covered, in a warm place for 5–10 minutes before serving.

la potée

2 oz salt pork
1 large onion
2 leeks
3 cloves garlic
2 oz bacon
¼ chicken
1 small turnip
1 medium-size potato
1 small head cabbage
6 cups light chicken stock
2 tablespoons chopped parsley
salt and pepper
1 lb green peas or lima beans, weighed in the pod (optional)
2–3 plain Italian-style pure pork sausages without paprika or fennel (optional)

SERVES 6–8

Cut the salt pork in small dice and fry gently in a pressure cooker, or heavy pan. Cook slowly for about 10 minutes, until it has rendered all its fat. Remove with a slotted spoon and reserve. Chop the onion and put into the pan. Cook slowly until lightly colored, adding a little extra fat if there is not enough from the pork. Finely slice the leeks, mince or crush the garlic, and add these. Cook for another 4–5 minutes. Cut up the bacon and add. Put the chicken in the pan and brown on all sides. Finely slice the turnip, potato and cabbage and add. Heat the stock and pour in, adding salt and pepper. Bring to the boil, and cook for 40 minutes under 15 pounds pressure (or simmer 2 hours). When the cover can be safely removed, cut the meat from the bones in small pieces and put back into the soup. Add more salt and pepper to taste, if needed. Pour the soup into a heated tureen. Sprinkle with chopped parsley and serve.

pasta e fagioli

½ lb dried haricot beans
¼ lb onion
2 oz carrot
1 oz celery
3 cloves garlic
3 tablespoons olive oil
½ lb slab bacon
2 oz spaghetti, broken in 1-inch pieces
grated Parmesan cheese
salt and pepper

SERVES 5–6

Put the dried beans into a pan with plenty of cold water to cover them, bring to the boil, turn off the heat and leave to stand, covered, for 1 hour. Chop the onion, carrot, celery and garlic. Heat the oil in the bottom of a pressure cooker and cook the vegetables gently for 6–8 minutes, stirring often. Drain the beans and keep the water. Add the beans to the pan, and make up the water to 1¾ quarts. Pour into the pressure cooker and put in the bacon and some black pepper. Add salt later if required. Bring to the boil and cook for 30 minutes under 15 pounds pressure; reduce pressure and remove the lid according to the manufacturer's directions. Test the beans to see if they are almost tender. If so, remove the bacon and spoon roughly half the beans into a food processor. Add the spaghetti to the cooker and boil gently for 12–15 minutes, not under pressure, until the pasta is tender. Chop the bacon in small cubes and stir into the soup, then add salt as needed. Stir in the pureed beans and simmer all the ingredients together for 2–3 minutes, then pour into a tureen and serve with grated Parmesan cheese. This soup can be made in an ordinary saucepan instead of a pressure cooker, in which case allow 1½ hours simmering.

chick pea soup

1 *cup chick peas*
2 *onions*
3 *carrots*
3 *leeks*
3 *stalks celery*
½ *lb tomatoes*
4 *tablespoons olive oil*
4 *tablespoons chopped parsley*
salt and pepper
SERVES 6

Cover the chick peas with cold water and soak for about 6 hours, or bring them to the boil, turn off the heat, and leave covered for 1 hour. Drain and cover well with fresh cold water. Clean or peel the vegetables and cut 1 onion, 1 carrot, 1 leek and 1 stalk of celery in small pieces and add. Bring to the boil, then reduce the heat and simmer until the chick peas are soft; this may take as long as 2 hours. Drain, reserving the liquid. Chop the remaining onion, carrots, leeks and celery, keeping them separate. Heat the oil in a heavy pan and add the chopped onion. Cook gently until pale golden, then add the chopped carrots, a few minutes later the leeks, and finally the celery. Peel the tomatoes and chop them, discarding the seeds. Add to the pan and stir in; cook gently for a few more minutes. Heat the reserved stock and add to the pan. Bring to the boil, reduce the heat, cover and simmer for about 20 minutes. Add the chick peas and bring back to the boil. Simmer covered for 5 minutes, then press everything through a coarse sieve. Reheat, adjust the seasoning to taste, sprinkle with chopped parsley, and serve as soon as possible.

lentil and pasta soup

6 *oz brown lentils*
2 *cloves garlic*
¼ *lb cooked ham*
1 *large onion*
1 *carrot*
1 *stick celery*
3 *tablespoons olive oil*
2 *oz spaghetti, broken into* 1-*inch pieces*
½ *teaspoon paprika*
salt and pepper
SERVES 4–5

Soak the lentils in cold water for 3–4 hours. Chop the garlic, ham, onion, carrot and celery finely. Heat the oil in a large heavy pan or pressure cooker and add the vegetables and ham. Cook them gently, stirring often, for 8 minutes. Drain the lentils, and add; stir until well coated with oil. Heat 1¾ quarts water (or light stock if available); add to the pan. Bring to the boil, reduce heat, cover and cook for 1 hour or 20 minutes under 15 pounds pressure. Reduce pressure until it is safe to remove cover, add the spaghetti, and cook normally, not under pressure, a further 12–15 minutes, until the spaghetti is just tender. Add salt and pepper to taste.

game soup with lentils

carcass of 1 *pheasant or other game bird (or turkey or duck bones)*
½ *lb brown lentils*
2 *onions*
2 *carrots*
2 *leeks*
2 *stalks celery*
1 *bay leaf*
3 *tablespoons olive oil*
salt and pepper
SERVES 6–8

Put the carcass into a large heavy pan. Cut in half 1 onion, 1 carrot, 1 leek and 1 stalk of celery and add with the bay leaf and plenty of salt and pepper. Cover with cold water. Bring slowly to the boil, reduce the heat, cover and simmer gently for 2–3 hours, or alternatively cook for 1 hour in a pressure cooker. Strain, and cool; remove the fat from the top after it solidifies. Measure the liquid and add water if necessary to give you 1¾ quarts. Chop the remaining onion, carrot, leek and celery. Heat the oil in a heavy pan and cook the chopped vegetables gently for 10 minutes, stirring now and then. Wash the lentils and add. Stir until they are well mixed with the vegetables and coated with oil. Heat the strained stock, and add. Bring to the boil, reduce the heat, and simmer for 45 minutes. Add salt and pepper to taste. This soup is also delicious when made with a whole pheasant. In this case, simmer the bird with the vegetables for 45 minutes only, then remove, and cut from the bones all the white meat, and return the bones to the stock and simmer for another 2 hours. Proceed as above, and finally, chop the white meat and add just before serving.

game soup with parsley

| 1 large onion |
| 2 large carrots |
| 1 medium-size turnip |
| 1 large potato |
| 4 tablespoons beef drippings or bacon fat |
| 5 cups hot, fresh or canned game stock (or turkey stock) |
| juice of ½ lemon |
| 4 tablespoons chopped parsley |
| salt and pepper |
| SERVES 5–6 |

Peel, then slice the onion, carrots and turnip very thinly indeed. Heat the fat in a large heavy pan; add the vegetables and cook them gently for 8–10 minutes. Peel and thinly slice the potato; add and cook for at least another 3 minutes. Add the stock, stirring, and salt and pepper to taste. Bring to the boil, reduce the heat, cover and simmer for 35 minutes. Leave aside to cool slightly; then pour, in at least 3 batches, into a blender and blend briefly. Reheat, adding the lemon juice and the parsley just before serving.

chicken barley soup

An excellent soup, filling and with an unusually fresh taste

| 4 leeks |
| ¼–½ cup pearl barley |
| 4 tablespoons (½ stick) butter |
| 6¼ cups hot chicken stock |
| 1¼ cups buttermilk or yogurt |
| juice of ½ lemon |
| 4 tablespoons chopped parsley |
| salt and pepper |
| SERVES 6–8 |

Soak the barley in cold water for 2–3 hours. Chop the leeks. Melt the butter in a large heavy pan, and sauté the chopped leeks for a few minutes, without letting them brown. Drain the barley and add. Pour on the stock gradually, stirring. Add salt and pepper. Bring to the boil, reduce the heat, cover and simmer for 1 hour. Beat the buttermilk or yogurt until smooth. If using yogurt, it can be mixed with a little cream for added richness. Add a ladleful of the hot soup, mix well, then add the mixture to the pan. Reheat gently, keeping below a simmer. Add the lemon juice to sharpen the flavor, more salt and pepper if needed, and the parsley just before serving.

peanut soup

¼ lb shelled peanuts
6 cups chicken stock
1 medium-size onion
1 large leek
1 small head cabbage
½ lb tomatoes
salt and pepper
SERVES 6

Chop the nuts coarsely and put into a heavy pan with 1¼ cups chicken stock. Bring to the boil, reduce heat, and simmer gently for 10 minutes. Slice the onion and leek, and quarter and slice the heart of the cabbage, putting the outer leaves aside for another use. Add to the pan with the remaining chicken stock, and add salt and pepper to taste. Simmer for 20 minutes. Meanwhile, peel and chop the tomatoes, discarding the seeds. Add tomatoes, and bring back to the boil; simmer for another 10 minutes, and serve.

almond soup

4 tablespoons coarsely chopped almonds
3¾ cups chicken stock
1 small onion
1 leek
1 stalk celery
4 tablespoons (½ stick) butter
1 tablespoon rice flour or potato flour
⅝ cup cream
pinch of mace
salt and pepper
SERVES 4–5

Put the chopped almonds in a heavy pan with the stock. Bring to the boil, reduce heat, and simmer for 10 minutes. Slice the onion, leek and celery. Melt the butter and sauté the sliced vegetables gently for 5 minutes, then add to the stock. Add salt and pepper to taste and simmer for 25 minutes. Put the flour into a small bowl, add 4 tablespoons of the hot soup; mix to a paste. Add to the pan and simmer, stirring, until smooth. Stir in the cream and add a tiny pinch of mace.

lettuce and almond soup

2 heads romaine lettuce
4 shallots or 1 bunch scallions
4 tablespoons (½ stick) butter
3¾ cups chicken stock
4 tablespoons cream
4 tablespoons coarsely chopped almonds
salt and pepper
SERVES 4–5

Wash the lettuces, and dry. Cut them across in thin strips. Chop the shallots or scallions; if scallions, use the best of the green part as well as the white. Melt the butter in a heavy pan and sauté the chopped shallots or scallions for a minute or two. Add the shredded lettuce and continue to cook gently in the butter for 3–4 minutes. Add the stock, and bring to the boil. Reduce the heat, cover the pan and simmer gently for 20 minutes. Blend briefly, or press through a medium-mesh sieve; return to the pan and reheat, adding salt and pepper. When hot, stir in the cream. Pour into a tureen, sprinkle on the nuts and serve.

potato and onion soup

1½ lb potatoes
1 large Spanish onion
4 tablespoons (½ stick) butter
3¾ cups chicken stock
1¼ cups milk and cream, mixed
2 tablespoons chopped parsley
salt and pepper
SERVES 5–6

Peel and slice the onion thinly. Heat the butter in a large heavy pan and sauté the onion slowly until soft but not browned. Peel and slice the potatoes and add to the pan. Pour on the stock, stir, and add salt and pepper. Bring to the boil, lower the heat, cover and simmer gently, about 25 minutes, stirring occasionally, until the vegetables are quite soft. Heat the milk and cream almost to boiling point, and stir into the soup. Adjust seasonings and remove from the heat. Leave for 5–10 minutes to allow the flavor to develop. (At this point the soup can be put in the blender, but I like it better as it is.) Reheat gently, and scatter the chopped parsley on top just before serving.

turnip and parsnip soup

½ lb turnips
½ lb parsnips
1 medium-size onion
½ lb carrots
4 tablespoons beef drippings, bacon fat or
4 tablespoons (½ stick) butter
4½ cups fresh or canned game stock
3 tablespoons sour cream
salt and pepper
SERVES 4–6

Peel and slice the vegetables. Sauté them gently in the fat in a heavy pan for about 5 minutes. Add the stock and bring to the boil; add salt and pepper. Reduce the heat, cover and simmer for about 30 minutes. Pour into a blender and blend, then reheat in a clean pan. Add more salt and pepper if needed, and just before serving, stir in the sour cream; heat through, but do not boil.

celeriac soup

1 lb celeriac (celery root)
½ lb potatoes
4 tablespoons beef drippings, bacon fat or
4 tablespoons (½ stick) butter
3¾ cups fresh or canned hot game stock (or turkey stock)
4 tablespoons sour cream
2 tablespoons chopped parsley
salt and pepper
SERVES 4–5

Peel the celeriac and cut in pieces. Peel the potatoes and slice thinly. Heat the fat in a large heavy pan, and cook the celeriac gently in it for 5 minutes. Add the potatoes and cook another 2–3 minutes, stirring around to coat everything evenly with the fat. Gradually add the stock, stirring as it thickens, and salt and pepper. Bring to the boil, reduce the heat, and simmer for 30 minutes. Blend briefly in a blender, in batches. Reheat, gently, adding the sour cream and more salt and pepper. Sprinkle on the chopped parsley, and serve.

consommé

1½ quarts stock from cooking pig's feet
1 lb stewing beef
½ lb tomatoes
3 stalks celery
SERVES 4

Remove all fat from the cold stock. Cut the beef in cubes and add; bring slowly to the boil. Simmer very gently for 1½–2 hours, then remove the beef; reserve for another dish. Cut the unpeeled tomatoes and the celery in pieces, put them into the pan and bring back to the boil. Simmer for another half-hour, then strain. For a delicate golden broth, serve this hot; or, chill and serve as a firm jellied consommé.

gratin of eggs and onions

6 *hard-boiled eggs*
2 *Spanish onions*
3 *tablespoons butter*
2 *tablespoons flour*
2 *cups chicken stock*
⅝ *cup cream*
½ *cup grated Gruyère cheese*
pinch of mace or nutmeg
salt and pepper
SERVES 4–5

Slice the onions quite thickly. Sauté them gently in the butter until soft, about 10 minutes. Add the flour and cook for another minute, stirring. Heat the stock and the cream and add; stir until blended, then simmer for about 15 minutes. Add the grated cheese, stirring until it melts; then add the salt and pepper, and mace or nutmeg. Preheat the broiler. Cut the eggs in quarters and place them in a shallow ovenproof dish. Reheat the onion mixture, then pour over the eggs, and brown under the broiler.

poached eggs on celeriac puree

4–5 *eggs*
1 *medium-size celeriac (celery root)*
¾ *lb potatoes*
4 *tablespoons (½ stick) butter*
4 *tablespoons cream*
3 *tablespoons grated Gruyère cheese*
salt and pepper
SERVES 4–5

Peel the celeriac and cut in pieces. Cover with cold water, add salt, bring to the boil, and cook until just tender. Drain well, and dry out over gentle heat. Peel and boil the potatoes, drain and dry out also. Press both vegetables through a medium-mesh sieve into a clean saucepan. Add butter and a little cream and stir over low heat, adding salt and pepper to taste. When smooth and well mixed, pour into a shallow ovenproof dish. Poach the eggs and lay them on top of the puree. Cover with the grated cheese and brown under the broiler.

curried eggs

8 *hard-boiled eggs*
1 *medium-size onion*
4 *tablespoons butter*
1 *tablespoon light curry powder*
1 *tablespoon flour*
2 *cups hot chicken stock*
⅝ *cup cream*
1½ *tablespoons lemon juice*
1½ *tablespoons orange juice*
2 *tablespoons chopped almonds or cashews*
SERVES 4

Chop the onion and sauté in the butter until golden. Add the curry powder and the flour, and cook gently for 2–3 minutes, then gradually add the stock. Stir as it thickens; when smooth and blended lower the heat and barely simmer for 10–12 minutes. Stir in the cream and the fruit juices. Add the nuts and stir until all is well mixed. Taste and add salt and pepper if needed. Cut the eggs in quarters; add them carefully to the sauce over low heat. Serve as soon as the eggs are hot.

smoked fish soufflé

1 *smoked haddock or other smoked fish (about 9 oz)*
1¼ *cups milk*
2 *tablespoons butter*
2 *tablespoons flour*
2 *tablespoons grated Parmesan cheese*
4 *eggs*
pepper
SERVES 4

Cut the fish in pieces and put into a pan. Add the milk and enough water almost to cover. Bring to the boil, reduce the heat, cover and simmer gently for 12 minutes. Lift out the fish and strain the liquid. Flake the fish, discarding all skin and bone, weigh 6oz exactly, discarding any extra. Melt the butter, stir in the flour, and cook, stirring, for a minute or two. Add 1 cup of the strained fish stock, gradually stirring as it thickens. When smooth, add pepper to taste. Stir in the grated Parmesan and the flaked fish. Pour the mixture into a blender. Separate the eggs and beat the egg yolks. Add to the mixture and blend. Pour into a bowl and leave to cool for a few moments. Preheat oven to 350°F. Beat the egg whites until stiff. Fold into the mixture in the bowl and transfer to a buttered soufflé dish. Bake for 25 minutes.

tomato and mustard quiches

¾ lb short pastry (see recipe, page 126)

2 eggs + 1 yolk

¾ lb tomatoes

⅝ cup heavy whipping cream

4 tablespoons grated Gruyère cheese

½ cup Dijon mustard

salt and pepper

SERVES 6

Preheat oven to 400°F. Make the pastry and roll out on a floured surface. Line 6 small quiche pans (3–4-inch diameter). Beat 1 egg yolk. Prick the pastry with a fork and brush with the beaten egg yolk. Put into the oven and bake for 5 minutes. Cool. Reduce the oven heat to 325°F. Peel the tomatoes, chop coarsely and discard the seeds. If very juicy, drain away the liquid. Beat two eggs in a mixing bowl with the whipping cream, and add salt and pepper to taste. Stir in the cheese and the chopped tomatoes, reserving a little cheese. Brush a layer of mustard over the bottom and sides of each pastry shell. Pour the mixture into the pastry shells and scatter the remaining cheese over the top. Bake for 15 minutes, until risen, and brown on top.

Jerusalem artichoke soufflé

¾ lb Jerusalem artichokes

4 tablespoons (½ stick) butter

3 tablespoons flour

⅝ cup milk

2 tablespoons finely chopped parsley

4 eggs

salt and pepper

SERVES 4–5

Scrub the Jerusalem artichokes, cover with lightly salted cold water and bring to the boil. Cook until just tender, about 15 minutes. Test with a toothpick. Drain, reserving a scant ⅝ cup of the cooking water. As soon as they are cool enough to handle, peel the Jerusalem artichokes and make a puree by pressing them through a medium-mesh or coarse-mesh sieve. Dry out the puree as much as possible by stirring in a pan over a gentle heat. In another pan, melt the butter, stir in the flour, and cook, stirring, for a minute or two. Combine the milk and the reserved cooking water. Heat this and add, gradually, to the butter and flour mixture. Stir until smooth; bring to boiling point, lower heat and cook gently for a few minutes. Preheat the oven to 400°F. Stir in the pureed Jerusalem artichokes and the chopped parsley and add plenty of salt and pepper. Separate the eggs and beat the yolks. Remove the pan from the heat and stir in the yolks. Then beat the whites and fold them in. Spoon into a buttered soufflé dish and bake for 20 minutes.

Fish/sea fish and shellfish

fish pie

1½ lb fillet of haddock or similar fish
1½ lb potatoes
7 tablespoons butter
3 cups milk
2 tablespoons flour
2 tablespoons cream (optional)
2 hard-boiled eggs
2 tablespoons chopped parsley
salt and pepper
SERVES 4–5

Peel and cook the potatoes in plenty of salted water until tender; drain. Mash to a puree, adding 4 tablespoons of the butter and 1 cup of the milk, and salt and black pepper to taste. Keep warm. Put the fish into a large heavy pan and add the remaining 2 cups of milk. Add enough water to almost cover the fish, and some salt. Bring to the boil and simmer until the fish flakes easily, about 10 minutes. Lift out the fish and strain the cooking liquid. Measure 1¼ cups and reserve this; keep the rest for a soup. When cool enough to handle, flake the fish, discarding all skin and bones. Melt 3 tablespoons butter, stir in the flour, and cook for 1 minute. Add the measured fish stock and stir until blended. Simmer for 3–4 minutes, adding salt and pepper to taste, and the cream, if used. Chop the hard-boiled eggs and stir these in with the flaked fish and reheat gently. Stir in the chopped parsley, and pour into a buttered soufflé dish. Spoon the creamy potato puree over the fish, and serve with broccoli, spinach, or a green salad. If made in advance, reheat very gently or the sauce will boil up and merge with the puree.

fireplace-grilled fish

For this you will need to arrange a grill in your fireplace
8 small (6–8 oz) rainbow trout or similar fish
2–3 tablespoons light oil
2 tablespoons melted butter
1 lemon
SERVES 8

Make two or three diagonal cuts on both sides of each fish with a sharp knife, and rub them all over with the oil. If you have a hinged double-sided sandwich-type grill it will need to be rubbed with oil too, to prevent sticking. Put the fish into it, and lay it on the flat grill in the fireplace. Allow 3–4 minutes for each side over a good fire. Turn onto hot plates and pour a little melted butter over each fish. Serve with lemon wedges. You will find the skin of the fish, charred by the heat of the fire, one of the most delicious things imaginable.

broiled fish on skewers

Serve as a first course or double the quantity and serve, on a bed of rice, as a main course
1½ lb any firm white fish, such as halibut
3 tablespoons olive oil
2 tablespoons lemon juice
1 small onion
1 tablespoon chopped parsley
2 lemons
SERVES 4

Cut the fish in small pieces and put into a bowl. Sprinkle 2 tablespoons olive oil and 1 tablespoon lemon juice over the fish and stir. Finely slice the onion and add, with the chopped parsley. Mix well. Leave for 3–4 hours. Thread the fish onto small skewers and broil carefully, turning often and basting with the remaining oil and lemon juice. Serve immediately, with lemon wedges.

gratin of mixed haddock

1 smoked haddock
¾ lb fresh haddock, filleted
1¼ cups milk
3 tablespoons butter
3 tablespoons flour
⅝ cup cream
4 tablespoons grated Gruyère cheese
salt and pepper

SERVES 4–5

Cut the smoked haddock in four pieces and put into a pan with the milk and enough water almost to cover it. Bring to the boil; lower the heat, cover the pan and simmer for 12 minutes. Lift out the smoked haddock and put the fresh haddock into the pan. Bring back to the boil, and simmer for about 8 minutes, or until the fish flakes easily. Lift out and strain the cooking liquid. Measure 2 cups of it. When cool enough to handle, flake all the fish, discarding skin and bones. Put them into a bowl, and mix together. Melt the butter, stir in the flour and cook, stirring, for 1 minute. Add the measured fish stock gradually, and stir until blended, then add the cream. Cook very gently for 3–4 minutes, adding salt and pepper to taste. Stir in the cheese. Add the flaked fish, and reheat gently. Pour into a gratin dish. Sprinkle with cheese and put under a broiler to brown.

baked smoked fish

2 lb smoked fish such as haddock
4 large tomatoes
4 tablespoons (½ stick) butter
⅝ cup milk
⅝ cup cream
2 tablespoons chopped parsley
pepper

SERVES 4

Preheat the oven to 350°F. Cut the smoked fish in large pieces (either whole fish or fillets can be used). Lay in a shallow ovenproof dish. Peel the tomatoes and chop them coarsely, discarding the seeds. Melt the butter in a sauté pan, add the tomatoes and cook briefly, stirring, over medium heat. Pour with their juices over the fish. Heat the milk and cream together in a saucepan, then pour over the fish and tomatoes. Sprinkle with plenty of black pepper and bake for 20 minutes. Serve sprinkled with the chopped parsley. Accompany with rice and a tossed green salad.

dressed crab

1 crab, cooked
2 hard-boiled eggs
5 or 6 scallions
¼ green pepper
1 tablespoon capers
2 tablespoons lemon juice
2 tablespoons chopped parsley
salt and pepper

SERVES 3–4

Buy a crab large enough for three or four people. Remove all the meat and mix the white meat with a little of the brown in a bowl. Shell the eggs, cut them in half, and remove the yolks. Chop the whites of the hard-boiled eggs, finely slice the white part only of the scallions and finely chop the green pepper. Add these to the crabmeat together with the capers. Add lemon juice to taste, and salt and pepper. Spoon the mixture back into the shell. Sieve the yolks of the hard-boiled eggs and sprinkle with the parsley over the top of the crabmeat mixture. Serve with thin sandwiches of brown bread and butter, or of watercress.

Fish/shellfish

stuffed clams

10–12 *large clams*
4–5 *shallots*
6 *tablespoons (¾ stick) butter*
1½ *cups soft bread crumbs*
1 *cup chopped parsley*
1 *tablespoon flour*
⅝ *cup half-and-half, or milk and cream, mixed*
salt and pepper

SERVES 4–5

Clean the clams thoroughly with a very stiff brush and several changes of cold water. Simmer ⅝ cup water (or wine and water mixed) and put the clams in to steam open; this should take 8–10 minutes. Remove the clams and set aside, reserving the stock. Mince the shallots. Melt 4 tablespoons butter in a heavy pan and sauté the shallots. When pale golden, remove the pan from the heat and stir in 1¼ cups soft bread crumbs. Spread the remaining bread crumbs on a baking sheet and put in a hot oven for a few minutes to brown. Remove the clams from their shells and chop them finely. Add them and the chopped parsley to the pan. Season with salt and pepper to taste. Melt the remaining butter and stir in the flour; cook, stirring, for a minute or two. Mix ⅝ cup of clam stock with the half-and-half. Stir over a low heat until thickened; then add to the clam mixture and stir in well. Spoon into half of the clam shells and press down to make neat mounds. Cover with the browned bread crumbs, dot with a little extra butter and put under a hot broiler until nicely browned.

moules gratinées

These may be served as a first course
1 *quart mussels*
2 *shallots*
4 *tablespoons butter*
1 *clove garlic, crushed (optional)*
1¼ *cups dry bread crumbs*
4 *tablespoons chopped parsley*
salt and pepper

SERVES 3

Clean the mussels thoroughly with a very stiff brush and several changes of cold water. Drop into ½ cup water, or wine and water mixed, cover and simmer for 4–5 minutes. When all have opened, remove them and cool slightly. Remove and discard one half-shell from each mussel. Keep the mussels warm in their remaining half-shells. Finely chop the shallots. Melt the butter and sauté the shallots until pale golden, adding the garlic (if used), halfway through. Add the crumbs and stir until all are lightly browned. Remove from the heat and stir in the chopped parsley. Moisten with two tablespoons of the cooking liquid and add black pepper to taste. Spoon a little of this mixture over each mussel, enough to cover the mollusk and to fill the shell. Place the filled shells in a gratin dish, dot with butter and brown under the broiler.

mussels in saffron sauce

2 *quarts mussels*
1 *shallot*
2 *stalks parsley*
1 *stalk celery*
2 *tablespoons butter*
1¼ *cups dry white wine*
1¼ *cups cream*
pinch of saffron

SERVES 3–4

Clean the mussels thoroughly with a very stiff brush and several changes of water. Chop the shallot, the parsley and the celery, including the leaves. Melt the butter in a broad heavy pan and sauté the chopped shallot, celery and parsley for 2–3 minutes, stirring. Add the mussels in their shells, then add the wine, and cover the pan. Cook gently over very low heat for 5–6 minutes, until the mussels have opened. As they open, lift them out and discard one shell each, leaving the mussels in their half-shells. Put them into a large tureen in a warm oven. When all the mussels are out, strain the stock into a clean pan, and boil up to reduce slightly. Heat the cream, add the saffron to it, and stir. Add to the stock, and season to taste. Pour three-quarters of the sauce over the mussels, and serve the rest in a separate sauce boat. Serve with rice.

seviche of scallops

Serve as a first course

8–12 *large scallops*
⅝ *cup fresh lime or lemon juice*
1 *tablespoon finely chopped shallot or mild Spanish onion*
1 *tablespoon finely chopped parsley*
1 *tablespoon olive oil*

SERVES 4

Wash the scallops and shells if you have some. Cut the scallops in slices ½ inch thick. Put in a bowl and cover with the lime or lemon juice. Refrigerate for 24 hours. Just before serving, drain off all the juice and mix the scallops with the shallot (or onion) and parsley. Add enough olive oil just to moisten. To serve, spoon into scallop shells or shallow dishes.

saffron shellfish salad

1 *quart mussels*
1 *lb cooked shrimp*
1 *cup rice*
pinch of saffron
4 *tablespoons olive oil*
4 *tablespoons lemon juice*
¼ *lb shelled peas*
salt and pepper

SERVES 4

Cook the rice in plenty of boiling salted water until tender; drain well. Bring ¼ cup water to the boil in a small pan; add the saffron and turn off the heat. Let stand for 3–4 minutes, then pour it over the cooked rice in a bowl. Mix well, then drain again. Dress while still warm with half the olive oil and lemon juice, adding salt and pepper to taste. Clean the mussels thoroughly with a stiff brush and several changes of cold water. Put them into a pan with 4 tablespoons water. Cover and lower heat to medium; steam 4–5 minutes. When all the shells are open, remove them from the pan and take them from their shells. Mix with the rice. Shell the shrimp and soak for 10 minutes in a bowl of salted water. Drain and add to the rice. Cook the peas briefly in a little boiling salted water; drain and add to the salad. Add the remaining oil and lemon juice, and salt and pepper to taste, stirring all together. Serve as soon as possible.

game pâté with chestnuts

1 *old pheasant*
1½ *lb belly of pork*
¼ *lb slab bacon*
2 *cloves garlic*
10 *juniper berries*
½ *lb chestnuts*
⅝ *cup stock*
2 *tablespoons brandy*
¾ *cup red or white wine*
1 *tablespoon coarse salt*
15 *black peppercorns*

SERVES 10–12 (SMALL PORTIONS)

Preheat the oven to 400°F and roast the bird for 15 minutes, then let it cool. Strip the meat from the bones leaving some scraps on the carcass for game soup. Chop the meat finely by hand. Cut a few thin strips of fat from the slab bacon, and reserve. Cut the belly of pork and the rest of the bacon in pieces and put through a meat grinder or food processor. Mix with the chopped pheasant. Put the garlic, salt, peppercorns and juniper berries all together in a mortar, and pound until well crushed. Add to the meat mixture. Shell the chestnuts and parboil them for 8 minutes in the stock, adding more stock if necessary. Drain, and chop them coarsely by hand or in a food processor and add to the mixture. Mix very thoroughly, then add the brandy and the wine. At this stage the mixture should be left for a few hours or overnight, to allow the flavors to develop. Then test for seasoning by frying a tiny ball, and tasting it. The pâté should be quite highly seasoned. Preheat the oven to 310°F. Lay the reserved strips of bacon fat diagonally across the bottom of two ovenproof dishes, or one large one. Spoon in the mixture, and pack it well. Place the dishes, uncovered, in a roasting pan half-full of hot water. Put into the oven and leave for 1¼–1½ hours if two small dishes; for one large one allow 1¾ hours. Take out and cool for a couple of hours; then lay a piece of aluminum foil on top of each pâté with a 2 lb weight on it, and refrigerate. This pâté tastes best if it is left for 2–3 days before eating. It will keep for a week in the refrigerator. If it is to be kept longer, seal by covering completely with a thin layer of melted lard; it will keep this way for as long as two months.

potted game

¼ *lb cooked game, preferably pheasant, grouse or partridge, white and brown meat mixed*
4 *tablespoons (½ stick) butter*
2 *tablespoons heavy whipping cream*
pinch of cayenne pepper
1 *sprig of parsley*
salt and pepper

SERVES 3–4

A food processor may be used to prepare this dish. Otherwise chop the meat finely and then pound in a mortar until reduced to a paste. Add the butter, cut in small pieces, and pound until smoothly blended in. Add the cream, salt, pepper and cayenne and mix together well. Pack into a small dish, and refrigerate. Garnish with a sprig of parsley.

pâté de campagne

1 *lb fat pork (belly or throat)*
1 *lb veal*
½ *lb pig's liver*
¾ *cup raw bacon, finely diced*
3 *cloves garlic*
16 *juniper berries*
½ *teaspoon mace*
4 *tablespoons brandy*
4 *tablespoons wine, white or red*

1 *tablespoon coarse salt*

16 *black peppercorns*

SERVES 10–12

Preheat the oven to 300°F. Put the pork, veal and liver through a meat grinder or food processor. Chop the bacon by hand. Mince the garlic. Put the peppercorns, juniper berries, salt, mustard seed, mace and garlic in a mortar and pound. Put the ground meats and the bacon into a large bowl, and add the garlic and spices. Mix well. Add the brandy and the wine and mix again. Fry a tiny ball and taste for seasoning; it should be quite spicy. Put into small ovenproof dishes. Preheat the oven to 300°F. Half-fill a roasting pan with hot water and set the dishes in it, uncovered. Put the roasting pan into the oven and bake for about 1 hour and 20 minutes. Cool; then put a piece of foil over each pâté and place a 2 lb weight on top. When cool, remove the weights and refrigerate overnight. Next day you could decorate the pâtés with bay leaves and cranberries, and cover each one with a layer of aspic, chilling again to set.

duck pâté

1 *duck*

¾ *lb fat pork*

¾ *lb veal (a cheap cut)*

¾ *lb slab bacon*

1½ *tablespoons soft green peppercorns*

2 *cloves garlic*

½ *teaspoon mace*

¾ *cup dry white wine*

3 *tablespoons brandy*

6–8 *thin strips fat bacon*

3 *small bay leaves and a few cranberries or juniper berries*

1 *tablespoon coarse salt*

SERVES 8–10

Preheat the oven to 400°F. Put the duck into a roasting pan and roast for 25 minutes. Let it cool. Grind the pork, veal and slab bacon with a grinder or in a food processor, together with the liver of the duck. Cut the meat off the duck and chop by hand in neat dice. Stir all together well and add the soft peppercorns, whole, and the garlic, crushed. Add the salt and mace, and the wine and brandy. Mix well. Leave for an hour or two. Preheat the oven to 310°F. Line the pâté dish with a few strips of fat bacon, placing them diagonally across the dish, or alternate them with red berries and bay leaves. Pack in the pâté mixture and place the dish in a baking pan half-full of hot water. Put in the oven for 1¾ hours. Cool, place a 2 lb weight on top of the pâté over a piece of foil, and set in a cool place overnight. The next day, remove the weight and refrigerate the pâté.

smoked salmon pâté

¼ *lb smoked salmon (buy lox trimmings if you can)*

½ *cup cream cheese*

4 *tablespoons (½ stick) butter*

1–2 *tablespoons lemon juice*

2 *tablespoons sour cream*

salt and pepper

SERVES 3–4

Chop the salmon and then pound in a mortar, or use a food processor. Beat in the cheese, a little at a time, and then the butter in small pieces. Continue to beat, or process, add the sour cream, then the lemon juice and salt and pepper to taste. Put into a small bowl and chill for several hours before garnishing with parsley. Serve with toast.

Pâtés/fish

smoked mackerel pâté

This pâté can either be served alone, with toast, or rolled up inside slices of smoked salmon, accompanied by lemon quarters

2 fillets smoked mackerel

½ cup cream cheese

1 tablespoon lemon juice

pepper

SERVES 3–4

Remove the skin from the fillets and weigh the flesh—you should have 4–5oz. Chop it finely and pound in a mortar or press through a sieve. Alternatively put all the ingredients into a food processor. Add the cream cheese, a little at a time, and then the sour cream, beating with a wooden spoon, or process, until all is incorporated smoothly. Add lemon juice and black pepper to taste.

smokie pâté

1 large smokie (smoked haddock)

½ cup cream cheese

1 tablespoon sour cream

1 tablespoon lemon juice

salt and pepper

SERVES 3–4

Weigh 3½–4oz of the smokie's flesh. Chop it finely, and pound in a mortar. Alternatively, use a food processor. Beat in the cheese, a little at a time. Add the sour cream, lemon juice and a little salt if needed. Add plenty of black pepper. Blend well. Put into a small bowl, and chill until quite firm. Garnish with parsley and serve with brown toast.

kipper pâté

1 plump kippered herring, or 4–5oz canned kippers

½ cup cream cheese

4 tablespoons (½ stick) butter

1 tablespoon lemon juice

pepper

SERVES 3–4

Unless you are using the canned, cook the kippered herring by covering it with boiling water and leaving it for 10 minutes. Scrape all the flesh away from the skin and bones and weigh 4–5oz. Chop this, then pound in a mortar or press through a sieve. Alternatively, you could put all the ingredients together in a food processor. Beat in the cream cheese and butter cut in small pieces, and add lemon juice and black pepper to taste. Spoon into a small dish and chill in the refrigerator until quite firm. Serve very cold, with whole wheat toast and lemon wedges.

shrimp pâté

½ lb shrimp, shelled

2–3 tablespoons lemon juice

4 tablespoons (½ stick) butter, at room temperature

salt and pepper

SERVES 3–4

Grind or mince the shrimps finely, reserving one for garnish, then pound them in a mortar. Alternatively, use a food processor. Add lemon juice and the butter in small pieces. Continue to pound or process until it is a smooth paste, adding salt and pepper to taste. Pack into a small dish, placing the one whole shrimp on top. Refrigerate for a few hours. Serve with brown toast.

Poultry/chicken and turkey

fireplace-grilled chicken

For this you will need to arrange a grill in your fireplace. Do not cook more than one chicken at a time in a normal fireplace

1 *small chicken, 2½–3 lb, halved*

Dijon mustard

olive oil

lemon juice

SERVES 2–4

About 1 hour before cooking, brush the chicken on the skin side with mustard. Pour over a little olive oil and lemon juice. When ready to cook, lay over a good fire, skin side upward. Cook steadily for 15 minutes, then turn over. Allow another 15 minutes for the other side. The outside will look quite charred, but will taste delicious. Serve with lemon wedges and a salad.

chicken stuffed with dried fruit

one 3½–4 lb chicken

½ lb mixed dried fruit: apples, apricots, prunes, peaches, pears, raisins (presoaked if not soft)

1 medium-size onion

6 tablespoons (¾ stick) butter

1 oz chopped almonds

salt and pepper

SERVES 4–5

Melt two tablespoons butter in a frying pan. Chop the onion and sauté it until pale golden. Chop the dried fruit after removing the seeds. Stir around for 2–3 minutes, then add the chopped almonds and salt and pepper to taste. Cool, then stuff the chicken with the mixture, leaving any extra stuffing in the frying pan. Truss or skewer the chicken to hold the stuffing in. Preheat the oven to 300°F. Melt the remaining butter in a casserole and brown the chicken on all sides. Sprinkle with salt and pepper. Leave the chicken on its side and cover the casserole. Bake for 1½ hours. Reheat the left stuffing and spoon it around the chicken on a heated serving platter. Serve with couscous, or rice.

roast turkey

1 turkey, 10–20 lb

stuffing (see recipes, page 106)

3 tablespoons softened butter

1 carrot, chopped

1 onion, chopped

1 stalk celery, chopped

½ bay leaf

salt and pepper

SERVES 10–20

Stuff the turkey. If possible, weigh the turkey after stuffing it, to allow the correct roasting time: 12 minutes a pound for a large bird (around 20 lb), 15 minutes a pound for a medium bird (around 15 lb) and 18–20 minutes a pound for a small bird (around 10 lb). Preheat the oven to 450°F. Arrange the bird, rubbed all over with butter and sprinkled with salt and pepper, sitting upright in a large piece of aluminum foil within a roasting pan. Fold the foil back to expose the breast. Put in the oven, and immediately turn the heat down to 350°F. Baste once or twice during the first 15 minutes, then wrap the foil completely around the bird until the last 15 minutes, when it can be removed to complete the browning. Meanwhile make the gravy: chop the carrot, onion and celery and put with the giblets (leaving out the liver) and bay leaf into water to cover; bring to the boil, reduce the heat, cover and simmer for 45 minutes–1 hour. Strain and reserve. When the bird is done, lift it onto a serving platter and cover with a cloth. Leave for 10 minutes before carving and serve with the gravy.

roast goose

1 *young goose*, 8–10 *lb*
1 *onion*
1 *carrot*
1 *stalk celery*
½ *bay leaf*
salt and pepper
SERVES 8–10

Only young goose should be roasted, so your bird should not weigh more than 8–10lb when ready for the oven. (The stuffing will add 1½lb to the weight.) Preheat the oven to 375°F. Put the goose upside down on an oven rack in a fairly deep roasting pan. Prick the skin all over with a cooking fork to allow as much fat to escape as possible. Put in the oven and allow 2½–3 hours roasting time for an unstuffed bird, 3–3½ hours for a stuffed one; or 20 minutes per pound weighed after stuffing. Baste fairly often. About halfway through the roasting time, reduce the oven heat to 350°F, and pour off the fat from the roasting pan. Meanwhile, cut up the onion, carrot and celery, and put in a saucepan with the giblets (excluding the liver), the half bay leaf and about 2 cups of water. Bring to the boil, reduce the heat, add salt and pepper, and simmer until reduced to a strong stock, about 1 cup. Strain this and reserve. During the last hour of roasting time, baste the goose often to brown the breast nicely. If it gets too brown, cover with a piece of lightly oiled aluminum foil. When cooked, remove the goose to a carving dish and pour off most of the fat from the pan leaving only a residue. Put the fat in a cool place and put the roasting pan over low heat, stirring as you add the stock to the residue of pan juices, to make a giblet gravy. Scrape all the juices and residue together, season with salt and pepper, and serve in a heated sauce boat. After the meal, the fat should be refrigerated until solid, then the bottom scraped free of all solid particles. The fat should then be reheated gently and poured through a strainer into jars, cooled, then covered and refrigerated, for future use.

stuffed goose neck

This dish is best made either after you have roasted a goose, or at the same time

1 *goose neck*
½ *lb pure pork sausage meat*
2 *oz bacon*
2–3 *oz scraps from roast goose*
1 *clove garlic*
¼ *teaspoon mace or nutmeg*
1 *egg*
salt and pepper
SERVES 4–5

Pull the skin off the neck, like taking off a light glove, so that it ends up inside out. Roll right way out, and sew up the narrower end with a needle and coarse thread. Finely chop the bacon and mix the sausage meat with the bacon and scraps of goose. (If you are making this before cooking the goose, the liver or some of the giblets could be substituted.) Crush the garlic and add, with plenty of salt and pepper, and the mace or nutmeg. Stir together. When well mixed, beat the egg and add; mix again. Push the mixture into the bag of skin. When fully stuffed, sew up the second end. Cook either in the roasting pan with the goose—in which case, add it about 1 hour before the end of the roasting time—or it can be cooked alone over medium heat, completely submerged in goose fat or lard, for 45 minutes. To be served cold, as an hors d'oeuvre, it can be cut in slices like a sausage. It is also good served hot with a puree of potatoes and cabbage, mixed.

duck in aspic

2 *ducks*
1 *large onion*
2 *carrots*
2 *stalks of celery*
4 *stalks parsley*
1 *bay leaf*
½ *bottle white wine*
2 *envelopes (½ oz) powdered gelatine*
1 *small orange*
1 *lemon*
salt and a few black peppercorns

SERVES 8–10

Cut up the onion, carrots and celery in large chunks. Put the two ducks into a casserole which just fits them nicely, and add the vegetables, and herbs and seasonings. Pour in the wine and enough water to half-cover the ducks, about a quart. Bring slowly to simmering point, removing any scum that rises to the surface. Cover and simmer gently for about 35 minutes. Turn the ducks over and simmer for another 35 minutes. Remove them and let cool. Cut the orange and the lemon in very thin slices. Strain the stock, measure about 3¾ cups, and let it cool. Add a little orange juice and taste for seasoning. Dissolve the gelatine powder in a little of the stock, then pour the mixture back into the stock. Strain again. Carve the ducks; cut the meat in neat strips, removing the skin. Pour a layer of the gelatine stock mixture into an oval dish. Lay thin slices of orange and lemon in the gelatine while it is still liquid. Put the dish in the refrigerator. When set, put a layer of duck pieces on top of the gelatine and cover with more gelatine stock. Refrigerate to set this layer. Build up the whole dish in this way; or fill up the dish with the sliced duck and pour the gelatine stock over it. Refrigerate overnight, then serve on a platter.

braised game birds

1 *pheasant, or 2–3 grouse or partridge*
1 *carrot*
1 *onion*
1 *leek*
1 *stalk celery*
3 *tablespoons beef drippings, bacon fat or butter*
1¼ *cups stock*
⅝ *cup red wine*
1 *teaspoon flour*
⅝ *cup sour cream*
salt and pepper

SERVES 3–4

Preheat oven to 310°F. Chop the carrot, onion, leek and celery. Heat the fat in a large heavy casserole and add the chopped vegetables; cook them gently, stirring, for 2–3 minutes. Push to the sides of the pan and put in the pheasant (or other birds) and brown quickly on all sides. Heat the stock with the wine and pour into the casserole. Add salt and pepper, cover the casserole and put into the oven. Pheasant will take 1 hour, grouse 45 minutes, partridge 35–40 minutes. Baste and turn the birds from one side to the other now and then. When done, remove from the oven and carve. Lift out the vegetables with a slotted spoon and put on a warm serving platter; lay the slices of game bird over them. Keep warm while you make the sauce: mix the flour into the sour cream in a saucepan. Measure ⅝ cup of the cooking liquor and strain into the sour cream mixture. Stir over gentle heat until slightly thickened and smooth. Serve in a sauce boat, with the game, or pour it over if you prefer.

Game/pheasant and pies

small game pies

It is best to use a pressure cooker for this recipe, but the birds can be roasted

1 *brace pheasants, or 2 grouse and 1 pigeon, or 1 pheasant and 1 grouse, covered with bacon*

8 *tablespoons (1 stick) butter*

2 *tablespoons brandy*

¼ *cup stock (or water)*

1 *stalk celery*

3 *stalks parsley*

1 *bay leaf*

3 *oz salt pork or slab bacon*

12 *pearl onions*

12 *tiny carrots*

4 *small leeks*

1½ *tablespoons flour*

¾ *lb short pastry (see recipe, page 126)*

1 *egg yolk*

salt and pepper

SERVES 6–8

Reserving 2 tablespoons of the butter, put 1 tablespoon inside each bird, and melt the rest in the pressure cooker. Brown the birds, then flambé them with the brandy. Cut up the celery, and add with the parsley and bay leaf to the pan. Add ¼ cup stock or water. Cover and cook 8–10 minutes under 15 lb pressure. Cool the cooker and remove the cover according to the manufacturer's directions. Lift out the birds and discard the vegetables, strain the juices and allow the stock to settle before removing the fat. Take the meat from the bones and cut in neat pieces. Put the carcasses back in the pressure cooker, cover with water and bring to the boil; add salt and cook under 15 lb pressure for one hour. Reduce pressure, remove the lid according to the manufacturer's directions and boil until the stock is reduced and well flavored. Cut the salt pork or bacon in strips, peel the onions, but leave them whole, cut the carrots in chunks, and thickly slice the leeks. Melt the reserved 2 tablespoons of butter in a heavy casserole and brown the salt pork or bacon, and the vegetables. Add the flour, and blend. Gradually add 1 cup of combined strained stock and juices from the braised birds. Cook, stirring until smooth, then add the cubed meat and mix. Let it cool while you make the pastry. Preheat oven to 375°F. Line 6–8 small pie tins with the pastry and fill with the meat and vegetable mixture, moistened with the sauce. Bake 25 minutes.

pheasant with cabbage

1 *roasting pheasant, about 2½ lb*

1 *small white cabbage*

6 *tablespoons (¾ stick) butter*

½ *cup stock (or water)*

salt and pepper

SERVES 3–4

Shred the cabbage and put into boiling salted water to parboil for 5 minutes. Drain. Put 2 tablespoons butter inside the bird and the rest of the butter into the pressure cooker, over a low heat. When the butter is melted, brown the bird on all sides. When lightly colored all over, remove the bird, pour off most of the butter from the cooker and reserve. Add the ½ cup stock or water to cooker. Place a rack in the cooker and the bird on the rack. Sprinkle with salt and pepper and cover with the shredded cabbage. Pour the reserved butter over the cabbage, then add more salt and pepper. Cover the pressure cooker and cook for 10 minutes under 15 lb pressure. Cool the cooker immediately according to the manufacturer's directions, and check the bird. If not done, cover and pressure cook for 1–3 minutes longer. Carve and lay on a platter with the cabbage.

Meat/beef

roast beef with Yorkshire pudding

1 *roast of beef*
⅝ *cup flour*
1 *egg + 1 yolk*
1 *cup milk*
pinch of salt

Sift the flour into a bowl and make a wide depression in the center. Break in the egg and the yolk. Put the milk in a pitcher. Start to beat the egg with a wire whisk, gradually incorporating the flour from around the edges, at the same time pouring in the milk in a slow stream. When all the flour is amalgamated, the milk should also be absorbed. Add a pinch of salt and continue to beat for a minute or two. Stand for an hour before using. Alternatively the batter can be quickly made in a food processor. To roast the beef, preheat the oven to 425°F. For a standing rib or roast sirloin, allow 10 minutes a pound. For smaller roasts, boned and rolled, allow 12 to 15 minutes a pound depending on the thickness; a thin sausage-shaped cut like a fillet will take less time than a square compact roast. Make sure it is really well wrapped and enclosed with fat. Place the meat directly on the oven rack two-thirds of the way up the oven, with an empty roasting pan underneath. (To prevent a dirty oven, line with aluminum foil.) Remove this pan briefly from the oven before the last 30 minutes of roasting time, pour off most of the drippings, leaving just enough to cover the bottom of the pan, and pour in the batter. Replace the pan under the meat and bake for the final half-hour. The only disadvantage of this method is that all the potential pan gravy is used up by the Yorkshire pudding. If preferred, just before putting the Yorkshire pudding batter in, the beef can be transferred to another roasting pan, and basted with a glass of red wine to mingle with its remaining juices during the last half-hour.

sea pie

2 *lb best stewing beef*
1 *large onion*
2 *carrots*
2 *tablespoons chopped parsley*
1½ *cups self-rising flour*
3 *oz shredded suet*
salt and pepper
SERVES 4–5

Cut the beef in small pieces and put into a heavy casserole. Add salt and pepper. Thinly slice the onion and carrots and add. Cover with hot water and bring to the boil. Reduce heat, skim and simmer, covered, over low heat for 1 hour. Meanwhile make the suet paste: mix the suet into the flour with the blade of a knife, adding a pinch of salt and enough cold water to make a firm dough. Roll out to about ½-inch thickness on a floured surface. Cut in a round slightly smaller than the circumference of the casserole, using the pot lid as a guide; lay this on top of the meat and vegetables. Replace the lid and simmer for another hour. To serve, cut the pastry in four or five sections, spoon the stew into a round serving dish, and lay the cut pastry pieces neatly on top.

steak au coriandre

2 trimmed loin or rib steaks, ½–1 inch thick

1 tablespoon coriander seeds

½ tablespoon butter

½ tablespoon light oil

1 teaspoon coarse salt

1 teaspoon black peppercorns

SERVES 2

Put the coriander seeds, salt and peppercorns into a mortar. Crush roughly with the pestle, mixing well. Coat two steaks with the mixture and leave for about an hour before cooking. Heat the butter and oil in a heavy frying pan and cook the steaks briefly over high heat, searing them for about 3–4 minutes on each side, depending on their thickness.

beef olives

5–6 thin slices round steak

½ cup shredded suet

2 tablespoons fresh bread crumbs

2 slices bacon

½ teaspoon grated orange peel

1 tablespoon chopped parsley

½ teaspoon chopped thyme

pinch of mace

1 egg

3 tablespoons butter

1 onion

1 carrot

1 leek

½ tablespoon flour

1¼ cups stock

salt and pepper

SERVES 5–6

Put the slices of beef between two layers of plastic wrap or waxed paper and beat with a mallet until very thin. Trim in neat rectangular shapes; chop the trimmings and add to the suet in a large bowl; add the bread crumbs, thyme, mace and salt and pepper. Chop the bacon and parsley and mince the orange peel, and add. Beat the egg and mix well with the other ingredients. Lay the beef slices on a flat surface and put a mound of the stuffing mixture on each one. Roll them up and tie with heavy thread or fine string. Slice the onion, carrot, leek and celery quite thinly. Melt the butter in a heavy frying pan and add the four vegetables. Brown them quickly, stirring constantly. Remove them, and put in the beef olives. Brown them quickly, turning on all sides. Remove them from the pan, and sprinkle in the flour. Blend, then add the heated stock, then blend again. Add salt and pepper to taste and replace the beef olives. Cover and cook gently for 1½ hours or until the beef is tender. To serve, cut the string and lay the olives on a bed of mashed potatoes. Spoon the sauce and vegetables over the top, or serve separately.

shepherd's pie

1 medium-size onion

6 tablespoons (¾ stick) butter

1½ lb ground beef

2 teaspoons flour

½ lb carrots

1½ lb potatoes

⅝ cup milk

salt and freshly ground black pepper

SERVES 4–5

Chop the onion and sauté slowly in 2 tablespoons butter in a heavy frying pan with a lid. When it starts to turn golden, add the ground beef and break it up with two wooden spoons. Cook slowly, stirring often, until browned all over. Stir in the flour and add 2 cups hot water. Simmer gently with the lid on, stirring now and then, for about

30 minutes, adding more water if needed. At the end of the cooking time, there should be a small amount of slightly thickened pan juices. Slice the carrots and boil until tender; drain, reserving, if you like, some of the carrot water for adding to the ground beef. Make the potato puree: peel the potatoes and cut in halves. Boil in plenty of salted water until tender, drain and dry well. Press through a medium-mesh sieve into the pan, and stir over low heat to make a dry puree. Melt 4 tablespoons butter in the milk, adding lots of salt and black pepper to taste. Pour into the potato puree, beating until all is smooth. When the meat is ready, spoon it into a serving dish and cover with the sliced carrots. Pile the potato puree over all, so that it covers the dish completely. Serve immediately, or reheat briefly in the oven if necessary, or brown slightly under the broiler. If made in advance, allow 35–40 minutes at 350°F to reheat. If preferred, a drier puree can be made by reducing the amount of milk, and the dish browned to a crispy crust under the broiler or in a hot oven.

stewed beef

It has taken me literally years to work out a recipe for stewed beef that I was really pleased with; the final period of cooking time produces a delicious caramelized effect on the top layer of beef, and a thick and tasty gravy. The choice of vegetables can vary according to the season; in summertime, I usually replace the turnip and celery with fennel and green peppers

2 *lb stewing beef*
1 *large onion*
2 *carrots*
1 *turnip*
2 *stalks celery*
2 *cloves garlic*
½ *cup flour*
2 *tablespoons butter*
2 *tablespoons olive oil*
2 *cups stock and red wine, mixed*
1 *tablespoon tomato puree*
juice of 1 *orange*
5 *sprigs parsley*
dash of Tabasco (optional)
salt and pepper

SERVES 6

Cut the beef in thin square pieces. Cut the celery, carrots and turnips in strips like matchsticks. Chop the onion coarsely. Crush the garlic. Season the flour with salt and pepper. Toss the meat in the seasoned flour, coating each piece. Heat the butter and oil in a casserole or heavy pan, and brown the meat rapidly on all sides over high heat. Remove the meat, keep warm, reduce heat a little, and put all the vegetables into the pan to brown. Stir around until they are pale golden, then replace the meat and stir in the tomato puree. Preheat the oven to 310°F. Heat the stock and wine in a saucepan—the proportions do not matter—and pour onto the meat with the orange juice, 3 stalks parsley, a dash of Tabasco, and black pepper. Cover and cook in the oven for 1 hour, then remove the lid and cook uncovered for another hour, stirring now and then. If the liquid reduces too much, replace the lid. To serve, lift out the meat with a slotted spoon and place in a shallow dish. Spoon the vegetables over it; pour over the sauce and sprinkle with the rest of the parsley, chopped. Serve with mashed potatoes and a green vegetable.

Meat/beef, pork and ham

beef marrow and dumplings

1½ oz beef marrow

1 egg

2 oz soft white bread crumbs

1 tablespoon finely chopped dill or parsley

5 cups beef consommé

pinch of salt

SERVES 3

Warm the marrow slightly in a large pan until it is semi-melted, then beat with a wooden spoon. Beat the egg and stir in. Continue to beat until smooth, adding a pinch of salt. Add the bread crumbs and the chopped dill a little at a time, mixing until it forms a firm soft dough. Leave in a cool place for 30 minutes. Form the marrow dough into tiny round balls, about as big as the top of your thumb. Bring the beef consommé to the boil, drop in the dumplings, reduce heat, and simmer for 4–5 minutes, covered. The dumplings will float to the surface when cooked. Test one to be sure it is cooked in the center. Drain, strain the liquid, then serve the beef consommé with the dumplings floating in it.

steamed meatballs

For this you will need a steamer, or one can be improvised. If using wicker steamers, one or two vegetables can be steamed at the same time on the other tiers. Alternatively, the meatballs can be poached gently in court bouillon or consommé

¾ lb ground pork and veal, mixed

1 small onion

pinch of cayenne pepper

4 tablespoons finely chopped parsley

1 tablespoon lemon juice

1 small egg

salt and pepper

SERVES 4

Put the meats in a mixing bowl. Finely chop the onion, and add, with plenty of salt and pepper, and the cayenne. (Since steaming tends to make food bland, add more seasoning than usual.) Stir in the lemon juice. Beat the egg and add. Mix well. Fry a small ball and taste it to test for seasoning. Shape into small balls on a floured board. Steam over boiling water, or stock, for 20 minutes.

pig's feet

1 pair pig's feet

1 large onion

1 leek

1 large carrot

3 stalks parsley

½ cup dry bread crumbs

2 tablespoons butter

1 lemon

SERVES 2

A day in advance, tie the pig's feet with string, so they will keep their shape. Put them into a pot with plenty of cold water and the vegetables, cut in large pieces. Bring slowly to the boil and skim carefully until no more scum rises. Add a little salt, reduce heat and cover the pan. Simmer gently for 3½ hours. Meanwhile, spread some dry bread crumbs on a tray and put them into a slow oven at 250–300°F. Stir the crumbs now and then until they are an even golden color, then remove from the oven. Lift the pig's feet from the pot and strain the stock, reserving it for consommé. Remove the string, cut the pig's feet in half, and roll in the crumbs to give an even coating. Refrigerate overnight. The next day, melt the butter, and paint the pig's feet with this. Broil them slowly, turning occasionally until nicely browned all over. Serve with lemon wedges.

pork scallops in cider sauce

1 *small loin of pork*
3 *tablespoons butter*
1 *onion*
1 *large cooking apple*
1 *cup chicken stock*
1 *cup cider*
1 *tablespoon cider vinegar or lemon juice*
4 *tablespoons heavy whipping cream*
2 *tablespoons chopped parsley*
salt and pepper
SERVES 5–6

Cut the meat carefully from the bone, in one piece, then cut in fine slices. Lay these between two sheets of plastic wrap, and beat with a mallet until thin. Heat the butter gently and sauté the scallops in batches, until golden on each side. Keep them hot, while the remainder are cooking. Meanwhile peel and chop the onion. When all the scallops are done, sauté the onion until golden in the same fat. Peel and core the apple, and slice. Add to the onion. When coated with butter, replace the pork slices. Heat the stock and cider together, and pour into the pan, adding the vinegar or lemon juice to cut the sweetness of the cider. Cover the pan and bring to simmering point, then cook gently for 35 minutes. Lift out the meat and arrange on a serving dish. Blend the apples, onion and sauce in a blender. Return to a clean pan, reheat, stirring in the cream. Pour over the meat and sprinkle with parsley.

pork chops with juniper berries

4 *large pork chops*
2 *tablespoons Dijon mustard*
8 *tablespoons juniper berries*
4 *tablespoons coarse salt*
SERVES 4

Crush the berries with the salt coarsely in a mortar, or in a food processor. Coat the chops with the mustard and press a layer of juniper berries and salt over each surface with a small knife. Broil slowly, turning carefully and trying not to dislodge the coating. Serve at once with a creamy puree of potatoes and a crisp lettuce salad.

boiled ham with parsley sauce

one 2½–3 lb ham, soaked overnight if very salty
1 *large onion*
1 *large carrot*
1 *leek*
2 *stalks celery*
1 *bay leaf*
3 *cloves*
2 *tablespoons butter*
1½ *tablespoons flour*
4 *tablespoons cream*
3 *tablespoons finely chopped parsley*
1 *hard-boiled egg, chopped*
pinch of mace
pepper
SERVES 5–6

Put the ham into a large pan, cover with cold water and bring to the boil. Unless you have soaked the ham overnight, repeat the process with fresh water. Skim off any scum that rises to the top. Cut up the vegetables in large pieces and add to the pan, with the bay leaf and cloves. Simmer gently for 1¾ hours, or until tender when the ham is pierced with a cooking fork. Lift out, slice and keep warm. Strain the cooking liquid. In a saucepan, melt the butter, blend in the flour, then add the strained stock and blend; cook gently for 3 minutes, adding mace and pepper. Stir in the cream, parsley and egg. Pour some sauce over the ham and serve the rest separately.

veal with apricots

6 *thick slices veal, about 2½ lb*
¼ *lb dried apricots, pre-soaked if not soft*
3–4 *tablespoons olive oil*
½ *Spanish onion*
2 *cloves garlic*
1 *green bell pepper, pith and seeds removed*
1 *red bell pepper, pith and seeds removed*
2 *oz fresh ginger*
pinch of saffron
½ *teaspoon cumin*
½ *teaspoon coriander*
2 *tablespoons butter*
1 *tablespoon flour*
juice of ½ orange
salt and pepper

SERVES 5–6

Brown the veal in the oil in a broad casserole.
Slice the onions, finely chop the garlic and the
ginger and cut the peppers in strips. When
the veal is lightly browned on both sides, add
the onion slices, chopped garlic, pepper strips
and chopped ginger. Add salt and pepper and
the saffron, cumin and coriander, and enough
hot water to almost cover the meat. Bring to
the boil, reduce heat, cover and simmer
gently for 1¼ hours, stirring occasionally.
Chop the apricots and add to the stew. Cook
for a further 15 minutes, or until all is tender,
then lift out the veal and put into a warm
serving dish. Lift out the vegetables and
apricots with a slotted spoon and keep warm
in a separate dish. Strain the sauce and reduce
if necessary by fast boiling. Melt the butter in
a clean pan and stir in the flour. Cook for
1 minute, then add the strained sauce. Stir
over gentle heat for 3–4 minutes, until
smooth and well blended, then add the
orange juice. Pour over the veal; scatter the
vegetables and apricots over the top. Serve
with a bowl of saffron rice, or couscous.

Lancashire hotpot

This excellent old English dish is made with
the same ingredients as Irish stew, but Irish
stew is cooked covered for the whole time,
usually on top of the stove, and ends up a
much more liquid dish

2–2½ *lb best-quality stewing lamb on the bone*
2–3 *tablespoons flour*
1 *lb onions*
1¼ *cups stock—chicken or beef, or made from the
lamb trimmings*
1½ *lb potatoes*
salt and pepper

SERVES 4

Season the flour with salt and pepper and dip
the lamb in the flour. Transfer to a buttered
casserole. (The traditional hotpot dish is deep
and round, but a shallower earthenware sort
can also be used.) Slice the onions and scatter
them all over the meat. Make either one or
two layers of meat and onions according to the
depth of the pot. Season each layer well with
salt and plenty of pepper. Add the stock.
Preheat the oven to 310°F. Peel the potatoes
and cut in thick slices; lay these over the
entire surface of the dish, overlapping to form
a sort of lid. Cover the pot and bake for
2 hours. Remove the cover, turn up the heat
to 350°F, and bake for a further 30 minutes,
until the potatoes are crisp and nicely
browned around the edges.

bargeman's dinner

Place a platform of sticks, or flat stones, in the
bottom of a galvanized iron bucket. Half-fill it
with water and bring to the boil over a bonfire
or simple stove. Fill a large earthenware jar, or
deep casserole, which has a lid, with layers of
lamb, cut in neat pieces with most of the fat
removed, and a selection of vegetables

cleaned and cut in large chunks: carrots, leeks, small whole onions, potatoes and turnips. Add salt and pepper to each layer, and a handful of pearl barley, distributing it evenly throughout the layers, together with plenty of chopped parsley. Pour in enough water to fill the jar by about two-thirds. Make a thick paste of flour and water to seal the lid completely and tie a piece of cloth over the top. Place the jar in the bucket, and after the water regains boiling point, allow 2½–3 hours' cooking time. Care must be taken to maintain a good heat, for the water must not go off the boil. A muslin bag, or even two, can be cooked in the pail at the same time. It could contain a pease pudding or perhaps navy beans; these should be soaked beforehand, and will take about 1½ hours to cook, so should be added about 1 hour after the stew.

moroccan lamb with pears

1½ lb boneless lamb

¼ lb dried pears (presoaked if not soft)

½ Spanish onion

1–2 green peppers

1–2 heads fennel

½ cup flour

3 tablespoons olive oil

¾ pint chicken or veal stock

2 tablespoons lemon juice

pinch of saffron

salt and pepper

SERVES 4

Cut the lamb in neat pieces. Slice the onion, cut the peppers in strips and the fennel in thin slices. Mix salt and pepper generously into the flour. Toss the lamb in the seasoned flour; then brown in the oil. Remove the lamb and add the vegetables to the pan. Stir while they cook gently until lightly colored. Heat the

stock. Put the meat back into the pan and add the heated stock. Add a pinch of saffron and salt and pepper to taste. Bring to the boil, reduce heat, cover and simmer for 1 hour. Cut the dried pears in strips, and add to the pan. Cook for a further 15 minutes until soft, then stir in the lemon juice. Serve with a bowl of couscous, or rice.

liver and bacon

4 thin slices calf's liver

8 slices bacon

1½ cups rice

6 tablespoons (¾ stick) butter

2 large onions

5 tomatoes

salt and pepper

SERVES 4

Cook the rice in plenty of boiling salted water until tender; drain well. Slice the onions. Melt 4 tablespoons butter in a heavy pan and sauté the onions slowly until well browned. Meanwhile, in another pan fry the bacon. Add the rice to the onions and stir until well mixed, adding salt and pepper to taste. When the bacon is crisp, remove it, add a little butter to the pan and fry the calf's liver briefly, about 2 minutes on each side. Remove the liver and bacon and keep hot. Cut the tomatoes in half and fry them in the same pan. To serve, put the rice on a platter and lay the liver and bacon on it, with the tomatoes around the edges. Serve with broccoli or green beans.

large sausage roll

1 *boiling sausage, about ¾ lb*

½ *lb short pastry (see recipe, page* 126*)*

1 *egg yolk*

SERVES 2–3 AS A MAIN COURSE OR
3–4 AS AN HORS D'OEUVRE

Poach the sausage gently by covering it with hot water in a pan which is long enough to allow it to lie straight. Bring to the boil and simmer gently for 50 minutes. Take it out and leave to get cold, when it will stiffen and be easier to handle. Meanwhile make the pastry and chill in the refrigerator. Roll out the pastry in a rectangle and lay the sausage on it. Trim it to fit and wrap loosely around the sausage, sealing firmly and decorating as liked. Beat the egg yolk and brush the pastry with this. Bake for 30 minutes at 350°F. Serve hot cut in slices, with foamy mustard sauce (see recipe, page 103).

toad-in-the-hole

This should be served with chopped cabbage, or a similar vegetable, and some good mustard

1 *lb pure pork sausages*

¾ *cup flour*

2 *large eggs*

1¼ *cups milk*

SERVES 4

The batter can be quickly made in a food processor, but if making it by hand, sift the flour into a large bowl and make a wide hole in the center. Drop in the eggs, and beat with a wire whisk, pouring in the milk in a thin stream with your other hand as you beat. Gradually incorporate the flour from around the edges into the beaten eggs, still pouring in the milk. When all is amalgamated, continue to beat for a couple of minutes, then stand in a cool place for 1 hour. Preheat the oven to 400°F. Beat the batter again thoroughly, then pour a thin layer into a rectangular baking pan which has been well greased and put in the oven for 5 minutes, or until set. Lay the sausages on it in one layer, then pour the remaining batter over them. Put in the oven for 30 minutes, then turn down the heat to 325° and bake for a further 15 minutes, or until the batter is crisp and well browned.

sausages with peppers

This excellent dish needs no other accompaniment, except possibly some good homemade bread

1½ *lb pure pork sausages, mild or highly seasoned, large or small*

1 *lb sweet peppers (mixed green, red and yellow, if possible)*

2 *tablespoons butter*

1 *tablespoon olive oil*

2 *shallots*

1 *clove garlic*

½ *tablespoon flour*

⅝ *cup white wine*

⅝ *cup chicken stock*

salt and pepper

SERVES 4

Heat the butter and oil in a heavy frying pan. Chop the shallots and sauté them slowly. Mince the garlic, and add. Cut the peppers in strips, discarding the seeds and pith. Add to the pan and cook slowly for five minutes, stirring. Push the peppers to the side of the pan and add the sausages, browning them quickly on all sides. Sprinkle in the flour and blend in over the heat. Heat the wine and stock together in a small saucepan and stir in. Cover the pan and cook gently for 15–20 minutes. Transfer to a serving dish.

sausages with beans

1½ lb large pork sausages

½ lb dried navy beans

2 tablespoons butter

1 tablespoon olive oil

1 medium-size onion

1 clove garlic

one 8 oz can peeled Italian tomatoes

salt and pepper

SERVES 4

Soak the beans for 3–4 hours in plenty of cold water, or put them into a pan, cover with cold water, and bring to the boil; turn off the heat and leave, covered, for 1 hour. Drain and cover with fresh water, bring to the boil, reduce heat, cover and simmer until tender, 45 minutes–1½ hours, depending on the beans. Add salt toward the end of the cooking time. When the beans are tender, drain the water off and reserve it for soup. Cover the pan and set aside until the sausages are cooked. Melt the butter with the oil in a heavy frying pan and sauté the chopped onion until pale golden. Chop the garlic and add it half-way through. Add the tomatoes, and chop them up roughly with a spatula. Brown the sausages quickly in another frying pan, turning until evenly colored, then add them to the pan with the tomatoes, and cover the pan. Cook slowly for 30 minutes, turning them from time to time and adding a little stock, tomato juice or water if the pan juices dry up. At the end of the cooking time, lift out the sausages and keep warm. Add the beans to the tomato sauce and cook gently for 3–4 minutes, stirring until well heated through. Add salt and pepper as needed. Pour the beans and the tomato sauce into a serving dish and lay the sausages on top.

sausages in vegetable sauce

1½ lb pure pork sausages

¾ lb leeks

½ lb turnips

¼ lb carrots

2 tablespoons butter

1 small onion

½ tablespoon flour

2 teaspoons Dijon mustard

⅝ cup cider

2 tablespoons sour cream

salt and pepper

SERVES 4

Parboil the leeks, turnips and carrots separately, but in the same water, until almost tender. Keep the cooking water. Chop the onion. Melt the butter in a heavy frying pan and sauté the onion, stirring frequently, until softened. Add the flour and the mustard and stir in. Measure ⅝ cup of the vegetable cooking liquid, mix with the cider and add to the pan, stirring. Chop the cooked vegetables coarsely in a food processor, or press through a coarse-mesh sieve and add to the pan. Stir them into the sauce and blend. Add salt and pepper to taste. Brown the sausages briefly in a lightly greased frying pan, and add to the sauce. Cover the pan and simmer for 20–25 minutes (or 30 minutes if the sausages are large), stirring now and then. Transfer the sausages to a warm serving dish. Stir the sour cream into the sauce, pour the mixture over the sausages, and serve, with boiled potatoes.

pork sausages

10 *oz lean pork (from the leg)*
10 *oz belly of pork*
1½ *cups fresh whole wheat bread crumbs*
⅜ *cup milk*
2 *cloves garlic*
12 *juniper berries*
¼ *teaspoon mace*
¼ *teaspoon allspice*
4 *large leaves fresh sage or* 1½ *tablespoons fresh basil, chopped (or if neither fresh herb is available, use* ½ *teaspoon dried sage and* ½ *teaspoon dried oregano)*
1½ *tablespoons chopped parsley*
2 *teaspoons coarse salt*
1 *teaspoon black peppercorns*
wide casings

MAKES ABOUT 1½ lb SAUSAGES

Cut the lean pork in cubes and put through a meat grinder, or use a food processor (the processor will give a better, coarser texture). Separate the fat from the lean belly of pork and grind or process the lean; chop the fat in tiny dice. Mix the meats together in a large bowl. Put the bread crumbs into a small bowl and pour the milk over them; leave for 10 minutes, then squeeze out the milk and add the bread to the meat. Mix well. Chop the garlic roughly and put into a mortar with the salt, peppercorns and juniper berries. Mash roughly with the pestle, only until coarsely crushed. Stir into the meat mixture and add the mace and allspice. Add the fresh or dried herbs and stir in. When all the mixture is well blended, test for seasoning by frying a little ball of it, and tasting. Then fill the casings according to the directions. These need slow cooking, either under the broiler, in a frying pan, or for 30 minutes in a 350°F oven.

veal sausages

These sausages can be broiled, grilled, fried or roasted. They are a trifle expensive to make, but extremely good for a treat. I like to serve them with a dish of brown lentils, or a puree of spinach, or creamed onions

¾ *lb belly of pork*
½ *lb lean veal, from the leg, loin or shoulder, ground*
2 *oz hard back fat, if available*
4 *tablespoons dry vermouth or dry white wine*
4 *tablespoons soft bread crumbs*
1 *tablespoon chopped shallots*
½ *teaspoon allspice*
¼ *teaspoon mace*
1 *oz natural pistachio nuts, shelled and roughly chopped*
2 *teaspoons coarse salt*
1½ *tablespoons soft green peppercorns*
wide casings

MAKES ABOUT 1½ lb SAUSAGES

Put the lean part of the belly into a food processor or through a mincer with the veal. Cut the fat part of the belly of pork and the back fat (if you have been able to get it) in tiny ⅛-inch cubes. Mix all the meats together. Pour the vermouth over the crumbs and leave for 10 minutes, then squeeze out and add the crumbs to the mixture. Stir in the chopped shallot, the salt, whole green peppercorns, the ground spices, and, lastly, the pistachio nuts. When all is well mixed, force into the casings.

candied sweet potatoes

6 *sweet potatoes or yams*
⅜ *cup light or dark brown sugar*
4 *tablespoons orange juice*
3 *tablespoons butter*
2 *cloves*

SERVES 5–6

Boil the sweet potatoes in their skins until tender, 30–40 minutes. Peel, and slice diagonally. Lay them in a buttered gratin dish. Preheat the oven to 375°F. Heat the brown sugar, orange juice, butter and cloves in a small saucepan and boil gently for 5 minutes. Remove the cloves and spoon some of the syrup over the potatoes. Put the gratin dish in the oven, and use the rest of the syrup to baste the potatoes while they bake for 30 minutes or until cooked.

spiced sweet potatoes

Buy the sweet potatoes with red or pink skins and white flesh if you can, rather than those with orange flesh

1 *lb sweet potatoes*
2 *tablespoons butter*
1–2 *tablespoons oil*
pinch of allspice
salt and pepper

SERVES 3–4

Peel the potatoes and cut in thin slices. Heat the butter and oil in a heavy frying pan and fry the slices, turning them frequently with a spatula so that they are nicely browned and even slightly burned in places. When soft, season with salt, lots of freshly ground black pepper, and a good sprinkling of allspice.

pommes Anna

1 *lb red potatoes*
3 *tablespoons butter*
salt and pepper

SERVES 4

Peel the potatoes and slice them thinly and evenly. Thickly butter a deep pie or cake pan. Preheat the oven to 350°F. Lay the slices of potato in overlapping layers, and dot each layer with butter, salt and pepper. When the pan is full, press the mixture down firmly and cover with a buttered piece of foil. Bake for 1 hour, and turn the pan from time to time so that the potatoes cook evenly. Turn out on a flat platter and serve in wedges like a cake.

hot potato salad

1½ *lb red potatoes*
2 *tablespoons white wine vinegar*
⅝ *cup sour cream*
1 *small onion*
3 *slices bacon*
2 *tablespoons chopped chives*
salt and pepper

SERVES 4

Boil the potatoes in their skins until just tender, and drain. Peel and slice them thickly while still hot. Stir the vinegar into the sour cream and pour over the potatoes. Stir gently. Chop the onion and cut the bacon in small pieces, and put into a frying pan. Fry briskly, stirring, until all is crisp and lightly browned; lift out with a slotted spoon and add to the potato. Add salt and pepper to taste. Scatter the chopped chives on top and serve as soon as possible.

potatoes dauphinois

1½ lb red potatoes
1 egg
2 cups milk
1 clove garlic, crushed
pinch of grated nutmeg
2 tablespoons butter
salt and pepper
SERVES 5–6

Preheat the oven to 350°F. Peel the potatoes and slice them thinly and evenly and place them in a bowl. Beat the egg, stir in the milk and the crushed clove of garlic, with salt and pepper to taste, and a little grated nutmeg. Pour over the sliced potatoes and turn them into a buttered gratin dish. Dot the potatoes with butter and bake for 1 hour.

parsnip and potato puree

Excellent with broiled steaks or lamb chops or roast meat. A puree of parsnips alone is delicious, but must be made with even more care to prevent it being watery

1 lb parsnips
1 lb floury potatoes (Idaho or Maine)
4 tablespoons (½ stick) butter
½ cup heavy whipping cream
salt and pepper
SERVES 4

Peel the parsnips and cover them with cold water in a heavy pan. Add salt, bring to the boil, and cook until just tender but not mushy. Drain well and dry out by stirring over gentle heat. Press through a medium-mesh sieve. Boil the potatoes, dry out also, then press through the same sieve on top of the parsnips. Mix together in a heavy pan, stirring over low heat until dry and blended. Stir in the butter in small pieces and add plenty of salt and pepper. Add the cream.

potato gnocchi

1 lb potatoes
4 tablespoons (½ stick) butter
1 egg + 1 yolk
½ cup + 2 tablespoons sifted flour
pinch of grated nutmeg
salt and pepper
SERVES 4

Peel and boil the potatoes, drain and dry them well, then press them through a sieve into a bowl. Add the butter, cut in small pieces. Beat the egg and egg yolk and add them with the flour, salt, pepper and a little grated nutmeg. Combine all ingredients well. Handle the mixture lightly and form it in little oval shapes about 1 inch long, and flatten slightly in the middle with a spatula. Drop a few at a time into boiling salted water and poach for 5 minutes, then lift out with a slotted spoon and drain on paper towels while you cook the next batch. Do not do too many at once. Transfer to a heated platter and cover with a tomato sauce. Serve as soon as possible with a crisp green salad.

green gnocchi with tomato sauce

1 lb spinach
2 tablespoons butter
6 oz ricotta cheese
¾ cup grated Gruyère cheese
2 eggs
2½ tablespoons flour
2 tablespoons butter
1 small onion
one 16 oz can Italian-style peeled tomatoes
pinch of sugar
salt and pepper
SERVES 3–4

Cook the spinach in a little boiling salted water until just tender; drain well. Chop the cooked spinach until reduced to a fine puree. Dry out as much as possible by stirring over gentle heat in a heavy pan. Cut the butter into small pieces, beat the ricotta with a wooden spoon; add them to the spinach with the salt and pepper. Then beat in the grated Gruyère cheese. When all is smooth, turn off the heat, beat the eggs, sift the flour and stir them in. Beat until smooth, then pour into a shallow dish and leave to cool. Put it, uncovered, in the refrigerator overnight. The next day it will have become thicker and more solid. If not, it means the puree was too moist; in this case beat in a little extra flour. Shape with two spoons, and roll lightly into miniature egg shapes on a floured board. Bring a large pan of lightly salted water to the boil and put in the gnocchi. Do not put too many in at once; they are better cooked in several batches. Lift out with a slotted spoon after 4–5 minutes, when they float to the top. Taste one to make sure it is cooked through. Drain them on a cloth, then transfer them to a shallow serving dish and keep warm, while you cook the sauce. Melt the butter and cook the chopped onion until a pale golden color. Chop the tomatoes roughly with the edge of a palette knife and add them. Simmer gently for about 12 minutes or until reduced to a mush, stirring in salt and pepper and a pinch of sugar. Pour over the gnocchi and serve.

Jerusalem artichokes mornay

1½ lb Jerusalem artichokes
generous ¾ cup milk
½ bay leaf
1 slice onion
2 cloves
4 tablespoons (½ stick) butter
3 tablespoons flour
⅝ cup cream
¼ lb grated Gruyère cheese
salt and pepper

SERVES 4–5

Brush the Jerusalem artichokes well under cold running water. Put them in a pan with cold water to cover. Add salt, bring to the boil, reduce heat, cover and cook until tender when pierced with a cooking fork. Drain, reserving ⅝ cup of the cooking water. As soon as the Jerusalem artichokes are cool enough to handle, cut them in thick slices and put them into a shallow ovenproof dish; keep warm. Gently heat the milk with the bay leaf, onion and cloves, almost to boiling point. Cover and remove from heat. Leave for 15 minutes. Melt the butter, stir in the flour, and add the reserved cooking water and the strained milk, gradually, stirring to blend. Simmer gently, stirring occasionally, until thickened and smooth. Add the cream, and salt and pepper to taste. Stir. Add the grated cheese, reserving a little to scatter over the top, and stir until blended with the sauce. Pour the sauce over the Jerusalem artichokes, sprinkle with the rest of the cheese, and put the ovenproof dish under the broiler to brown. Alternatively, you could prepare this dish in advance and reheat for 20–25 minutes in a preheated oven at 400°F.

Vegetables/greens, peas and beans

cabbage with cumin

1 *head cabbage*
1 *cup milk*
1 *tablespoon butter*
⅓ *teaspoon ground cumin*
salt and pepper
SERVES 4

Use only the tender inner section of a green cabbage. Thinly slicé it and cook it in a heavy pan with enough milk to barely cover it. Simmer very gently, until the cabbage is soft. Add the butter, salt, pepper and the ground cumin before serving.

green pancakes with tomato filling

¼ *lb spinach*
¼ *lb flour*
1 *egg*
⅝ *cup milk*
pinch of salt
1 *lb tomatoes*
2 *tablespoons butter*
2 *teaspoons flour*
pinch of sugar
⅝ *cup sour cream*
salt and pepper
SERVES 4–5

Make the batter at least an hour in advance of your cooking time. If you have a juice extractor, put the spinach in this; it should give you approximately 4 tablespoons spinach juice. If not, cook the spinach and press it through a fine-mesh sieve with enough of the cooking water to give you a very thin puree; measure 4 tablespoons of this and cool it. Put the flour into a bowl and make a hole in the center. Add a pinch of salt and break the egg into the hole. Beat with a whisk, drawing flour from the edges gradually into the center, at the same time gradually pouring in the milk. When all the milk is absorbed, add the spinach juice and beat until amalgamated. (Alternatively the batter can be quickly made in a food processor.) Let stand for an hour before using. Meanwhile make the filling: peel and chop the tomatoes and sauté them for about 5 minutes, in the butter. Shake the flour into the pan and stir until amalgamated, then add the salt, pepper and sugar. Stir in the sour cream and cook gently until blended and heated, stirring continuously. Cover and put aside in a warm place. Beat the batter thoroughly and make about 10 small pancakes. Put a spoonful of filling on each and roll them up. Serve immediately.

pease pudding

This is delicious when served with sausages or boiled ham

½ *lb split peas or whole dried peas*
3 *tablespoons butter*
1 *large egg*
1 *or 2 pieces bacon or salt pork (optional)*
salt and pepper
SERVES 4

Split peas do not need soaking, but if you are using whole dried peas, soak them for 3–4 hours first. Cover the peas with lightly salted water in a heavy pot and cook until tender, or tie them loosely in a muslin bag and cook in the same pot as a piece of bacon or salt pork for 1–1½ hours, or until soft. Drain them well and press through a coarse-mesh sieve, or put in a food processor. Cut the butter in small pieces, beat the egg and add to the peas. Season well with plenty of salt and freshly ground black pepper. Form the mixture in a ball, wrap it tightly in a muslin cloth and tie with a string, leaving long ends to lift it in and out of the pan. Lower the bag into a heavy pan of fast-boiling water, preferably with a piece of bacon or salt pork already cooking in it, and cook for 1 hour. To serve, untie the cloth and turn the pudding out carefully into a round dish.

three-bean salad

¼ lb dried navy beans
½ lb green dried flageolets
¼ lb red kidney beans
2½ tablespoons olive oil
1 tablespoon white wine vinegar
1 Spanish onion
4 tablespoons chopped parsley
salt and pepper

SERVES 4–6

Each of the three types of bean must be cooked separately. Either soak them in separate bowls for 2–3 hours, or bring them to the boil in a heavy pan, covered with cold water. Turn off the heat and leave covered for 1 hour. Then drain away the water, cover with fresh cold water and cook until tender, adding salt only toward the end of the cooking. When the beans are tender, drain them in a colander and rinse them briefly under cold running water. Mix all the beans together in a bowl and add salt and pepper. Add enough olive oil to moisten well without leaving a pool in the bottom of the bowl, and about one-third as much wine vinegar. Cut the Spanish onion in quarters, then cut each piece in thin slices, and divide each slice in thin strips. Stir into the beans and mix well. Add the chopped parsley, stirring in some of it, and leaving some on top as a garnish. This salad is best eaten within an hour or so of cooking, before it has completely cooled.

vegetarian casserole

4–5 oz buckwheat or couscous
2 tablespoons light oil
2 tablespoons butter
1 large onion
2 leeks
2 carrots
3 zucchini squash
½ lb tomatoes
1 egg
1 tablespoon flour
1¼ cups yogurt
salt and pepper

SERVES 4

Cook the buckwheat or couscous according to the directions on the packet. Put the cooked buckwheat or couscous in the bottom of a buttered casserole. Slice the onion and leeks. Heat the oil and butter in a frying pan and sauté the onion and leeks until soft and lightly colored. Slice the carrots and parboil them until almost tender; drain. Chop the unpeeled zucchini and add to the onion and leeks; cover the pan and simmer gently for 4 minutes, then add the sliced carrots and a little of their cooking water. Cook gently for another 3–4 minutes. Peel and thickly slice the tomatoes and add. Cook very briefly, then season well with salt and pepper, and pour into the casserole over the buckwheat or couscous. Preheat the oven to 350°F. Beat the egg, stir in the flour, add the yogurt and mix well. Add salt and pepper, and pour into the casserole over the vegetables. Cover the pan and bake for 30 minutes. Serve with a green salad.

beans with garlic butter

This is a delicious accompaniment to a casserole of beef, with a simple lettuce salad

½ lb kidney, navy or lima beans

1 onion

1 carrot

1 stalk celery

½ bay leaf

½ cup (1 stick) unsalted butter at room temperature

2 cloves garlic

2 tablespoons finely chopped parsley and a few parsley stalks

1–2 tablespoons lemon juice

salt and pepper

SERVES 4–5

Put the beans into a saucepan and cover generously with cold water. Bring them slowly to the boil, turn off the heat, cover the pan and leave for 1 hour. Alternatively, soak the beans for 3–4 hours. In either case, throw away the water, cover with fresh cold water, add the halved onion, carrot and celery, the bay leaf and a few parsley stalks. Bring to the boil and simmer until tender, adding some salt toward the end of the cooking. Meanwhile make the garlic butter. Pound the butter in a mortar until it is a smooth cream, or cream it in a bowl with the back of a wooden spoon. Alternatively it can be quickly made in a food processor. Put the garlic into a press, or chop it very finely, and add to the butter. Continue pounding until amalgamated into a smooth paste. Add the finely chopped parsley, lemon juice to taste, and freshly ground black pepper. Form in a ball and chill in the refrigerator until needed. When the beans are tender, drain them and discard the flavoring vegetables. Put the beans into a clean pan and reheat, stirring in the garlic butter in small pieces.

curried lentils

Yellow split peas are also excellent cooked in this way. Curried lentils are good with broiled sausages, hot boiled ham, or hard-boiled eggs

½ lb lentils

2 onions

3 tablespoons oil

1 clove garlic, crushed

1 teaspoon garam masala (ground Indian spice mixture)

½ teaspoon mustard seed

½ teaspoon ground turmeric

½ teaspoon ground ginger

¼ teaspoon chili powder

a few fresh coriander leaves (cilantro), or

½ teaspoon ground coriander

salt

SERVES 3–4

Pick over the lentils carefully and put them into a saucepan with 5 cups of cold water. Bring to the boil and simmer until the lentils are soft, the water almost boiled away. Add some salt halfway through the cooking. Slice the onions, heat the oil in a frying pan and fry the onions until soft and golden. Add the garlic and spices and cook another 5 minutes, stirring often. When the lentils are ready – reduced to a thick soupy consistency – stir in the onions, garlic and spices. Reheat, stirring all the time. When available, chop a few fresh coriander leaves and add at this stage. Otherwise add ½ teaspoon ground coriander with the other spices.

lentil vinaigrette with sausage

½ lb lentils
¼ Spanish onion
3 tablespoons olive oil
1 tablespoon white wine vinegar
2 pepperoni, kabanos or frankfurter sausages
salt and pepper

SERVES 2–3

Put the lentils into a pan with water to cover; bring to the boil, then reduce the heat and simmer until tender. Meanwhile cut the onion in thin slices. Drain the lentils well. While they are still hot, add salt and pepper to taste, and stir in the onions. Add the oil and vinegar, and mix well. Cut the sausages in fairly thick slices and stir into the lentils, scattering some over the top. If using frankfurters, heat them first by pouring boiling water over them, let stand for 5 minutes, then drain and slice. This dish should be served as soon as possible after making, while still warm.

spiced lentils

These are good served with bacon and hot hard-boiled eggs
½ lb brown lentils
1 medium-size onion
3 tablespoons butter
1 large clove garlic
1 teaspoon ground coriander
½ teaspoon ground cumin
½ teaspoon ground ginger
¼ teaspoon chili powder
¼ teaspoon ground turmeric
½ teaspoon salt

SERVES 3–4

Chop the onion. Melt the butter in a large frying pan and sauté the onion gently. Crush the garlic and add with the five spices.

Carefully pick over, wash and drain the lentils and add them to the pan. Stir. Cook for 5 minutes, stirring now and then. Add 3¾ cups hot water and stir. Cover the pan, and simmer for about 35 minutes, or until the lentils are soft and the water all absorbed. Taste, and add salt and more spices, if needed for extra flavor, before serving.

Esau's potage (a lentil and rice stew)

This comforting dish, the Biblical "mess of pottage," is an excellent accompaniment to sausages, hard-boiled eggs, ham steaks or broiled pork chops
½ lb brown lentils
¼ lb long grain rice
1 large onion
3 tablespoons olive oil
1 tablespoon salt

SERVES 4

Pick over the lentils well, and put them into a heavy pan with 5 cups salted water. Bring to the boil, reduce heat, cover and simmer gently for about 35 minutes, or until the lentils are nearly tender. Put the rice in a colander, rinse under cold running water, drain and add to the pan. Bring to the boil, reduce heat and simmer until both the rice and lentils are soft. Meanwhile chop the onion, and fry it in the oil until pale golden; add to the pan before the final 5–10 minutes cooking time. It may be necessary to add a little extra water if the dish gets too thick. This is best eaten immediately, but is also good eaten warm, or even cold. In the latter case, however, it must be thinned down considerably, for it is inclined to thicken when it cools.

hummus

½ lb chick-peas
1–2 cloves garlic
⅝ cup tahini (sesame seed paste)
½ cup lemon juice
1 tablespoon olive oil or sesame seed oil
pinch of paprika
salt and pepper
SERVES 4–6

Soak the chick-peas for 6–8 hours or overnight. Drain them and cover with plenty of fresh cold water in a heavy pan. Bring to the boil and simmer for 2 hours or until they are soft. Keep an eye on them as it may be necessary to add more water from time to time. Add some salt after about 1 hour. When soft, drain them and keep the cooking stock. Press them through a medium-mesh sieve, or pound to a paste in a mortar. Alternatively this can be done very quickly in a food processor. Add some of the cooking liquid to thin the mixture, which should be about the same consistency as thick cream. Crush the garlic and beat it into the paste, then add the tahini and lemon juice alternately a little at a time, beating in each addition until blended. When the mixture is well blended, taste for seasoning and add salt if needed. Adjust the consistency by adding more stock if required, then pour into a very shallow dish. Pour a thin film of olive oil or sesame seed oil over the top and sprinkle with paprika. Serve with hot pita bread. Hummus keeps well and if made in advance should be kept in a covered jar in the refrigerator with a film of oil (or oiled waxed paper) over the top. Before serving, beat the oil into the puree, spread on a dish and cover with a fresh film of oil.

fruit and vegetable curry

1 medium-size onion
4 tablespoons (½ stick) butter
1 tablespoon light curry powder
1 tablespoon flour
2 cups chicken or vegetable stock
2 tablespoons lemon juice
2 tablespoons orange juice
1 tablespoon red currant or crabapple jelly
1 oz almonds, coarsely chopped
3 firm bananas
½ honeydew melon
½ lb tomatoes
SERVES 4–6

Chop the onion; melt the butter in a large frying pan and sauté the onion gently until golden; add the curry powder and flour and stir for 2–3 minutes. Heat the stock and add it gradually, stirring until blended, then simmer gently for 10–12 minutes, stirring now and then. Press the jelly through a small sieve and add it to the pan with the fruit juices and the nuts. Simmer for another 3 minutes. Cut the bananas in thick slices, and the melon in cubes, and add to the pan. Peel the tomatoes, cut them in eighths, and add, stirring in. Simmer the mixture for a few moments, until all is well heated and mixed. Serve with rice.

mayonnaise

2 egg yolks, at room temperature
pinch of salt
pinch of mustard powder
1¼ cups olive oil
1½ tablespoons white wine vinegar
½ tablespoon lemon juice

MAKES ABOUT 1½ CUPS

Place the egg yolks in a large bowl, firmly anchored on a damp cloth so that it will not slide around. Add the salt and mustard powder. Break and stir the yolks with a wire whisk, then start adding the oil, literally drop by drop, beating all the time. After a moment or two the mixture will start to take on an emulsified appearance, like a thick ointment; now you can start to add the oil a little more quickly, in a very thin stream, beating constantly with the other hand. After half the oil is absorbed, the remainder can be added in a thin steady stream. Add a little of the vinegar from time to time. When all the oil is used up, add what is left of the vinegar, and the lemon juice. Keep in a cool place until needed, covered tightly with plastic wrap. The quantities can easily be doubled, but do not try to make half this amount, as it is likely to separate. If the sauce does separate, start again in a clean bowl, either by breaking in a fresh egg yolk, or a teaspoonful of Dijon mustard. Then add the separated sauce, drop by drop, then the remaining ingredients. Additions of chopped herbs or other ingredients should be stirred in at the very last; the sauce can be lightened by folding in a spoonful of whipped cream at the end. For mustard mayonnaise, add 1 tablespoon Dijon mustard instead of mustard powder and stir in 4 tablespoons sour cream at the end.

foamy mustard sauce

Serve with pork sausages or pork chops
2 tablespoons butter
1½ tablespoons flour
2 cups milk
1½ teaspoons Dijon mustard
1 teaspoon white wine vinegar
1 teaspoon lemon juice
2 tablespoons heavy whipping cream
1 egg white
salt and pepper

Melt the butter, stir in the flour and cook, stirring, 1–2 minutes. Add the mustard and stir until smooth. Heat the milk and add; stir until blended. Add salt and pepper to taste, then add the vinegar and lemon juice. Stir in the cream. Pour into a bowl and cool for a moment while you beat the egg white. When the egg is stiff, fold it into the sauce and serve as soon as possible.

apple and horseradish sauce

Serve with cold roast goose, duck or pork
2 cooking apples
⅝ cup sour cream
3–4 tablespoons grated horseradish
1 teaspoon lemon juice

Make an unsweetened puree of the apples by stewing them in a little water, then pressing them through a coarse-mesh sieve. Cool; then stir in the sour cream. Gradually add the grated horseradish, a spoonful at a time, stopping when the flavor is strong enough. The apple and horseradish flavors should be evenly balanced so that neither predominates. Add the lemon juice, chill and serve.

Sauces/fruit and nut

applesauce

Serve hot, warm or cold, with sausages, pork chops, roast pork or duck

2 *cooking apples*

1 *tablespoon sugar*

1 *teaspoon lemon juice*

Peel and core the apples and cut them in thick slices. Put them in a small pan with just enough water to cover the bottom. Add the sugar and simmer until the apples are soft and mushy. Stir in the lemon juice. Either leave as it is, breaking up the apples with the edge of a wooden spoon, or press through a sieve; or, for a really smooth sauce, put the mixture in a blender, adding a little butter if you like.

cranberry sauce

Serve with hot or cold roast turkey, goose, duck, or chicken; also good with hot or cold ham or pork

½ *lb fresh cranberries*

½ *cup sugar*

1 *tablespoon orange juice*

1 *teaspoon grated orange peel*

Pick over the berries and wash well. Put 1¼ cups water in a heavy pan with the sugar and bring to the boil. Stir until the sugar has melted. Add the berries and simmer for about 3 minutes, or until the berries start to burst. Cover the pan and remove from the heat. Leave for about 15 minutes, then pour into a bowl and add the orange juice and peel. Mix well. When completely cold, put in the refrigerator. This sauce will keep for weeks if refrigerated in a covered jar.

cherry sauce

Serve hot or cold with duck, goose, turkey, hot or cold ham or spiced beef

1 *can (½–¾ lb) black cherries*

⅝ *cup port or other red wine*

peel of ½ lemon

peel of 1 orange

3 *tablespoons red currant jelly*

1 *tablespoon Dijon mustard*

2 *tablespoons lemon juice*

2 *tablespoons orange juice*

Cut the peel from the lemon and orange in thin strips with a sharp potato peeler. Drain the juice from the black cherries (put aside for another use) and remove the seeds, if any. Put the cherries in a pan with the wine and add the lemon and orange peel. Simmer for 10 minutes, until quite thick and syrupy. Meanwhile melt the jelly in a small heatproof bowl over boiling water. Stir in the mustard, then the lemon and orange juices. When the cherries are done, remove them from the heat and press the jelly mixture through a sieve into the pan with the cherries; mix well.

plum sauce

Serve either hot or cold with roast duck, goose, turkey, hot or cold ham or spiced beef

one 1 lb can plums

⅝ *cup port or other red wine (preferably sweet)*

¼ *teaspoon ground cinnamon*

¼ *teaspoon ground cloves*

¼ *teaspoon ground nutmeg*

¼ *teaspoon ground ginger*

3 *tablespoons red currant or crabapple jelly*

1 *tablespoon Dijon mustard*

1 *tablespoon orange juice*

Drain the juice from the plums and remove the seeds, if any. Put in a pan with the wine. Add the four spices. Simmer for 10 minutes, until slightly thick and jammy. Meanwhile melt the jelly in a small heatproof bowl over boiling water, and stir in the mustard and the orange juice. Press the mixture through a sieve into the pan with the plums; cool. The sauce may be used immediately or stored for a week or two in the refrigerator.

Malaysian nut sauce

Serve with broiled chicken pieces or small skewers of lamb or pork

1 *cup unsalted peanuts*

2 *tablespoons oil*

1 *medium-size onion*

one 3½–4 oz *package shredded or flaked coconut*

1 *tablespoon soft brown sugar*

1 *tablespoon soy sauce*

1½–2 *tablespoons lemon juice*

2–3 *dashes Tabasco*

salt and pepper

Heat ½ tablespoon oil in a frying pan and fry the nuts until a golden brown, then chop them coarsely by hand or in a food processor. Chop the onion finely and fry in the remaining oil until pale golden; add to the nuts and blend. Pour 1¼ cups water over the shredded or flaked coconut and leave for 20–30 minutes; blend quickly in a blender or food processor (after removing the nuts) and pour through a coarse strainer into a saucepan. Heat, adding the chopped nuts and onions, the sugar, soy sauce, 1 tablespoon lemon juice, a dash of Tabasco and salt and pepper to taste. Bring to the boil, reduce heat and simmer for 5 minutes, adding a little water if it gets too thick. Add more lemon juice and Tabasco as required. Serve hot with rice.

Cumberland sauce

Serve with any kind of cold meat, especially ham, game, cold meat loaf or pâté

1 *shallot or small onion*

2 *oranges*

1 *lemon*

¾ *cup red currant jelly*

1 *teaspoon Dijon mustard*

⅝ *cup port*

2 *teaspoons arrowroot*

Chop the shallot or the onion finely, and put into a small saucepan. Cut the peel from the lemon and 1 orange in thin strips and add to the shallot or onion in the pan. Cover with cold water, bring to the boil, reduce heat, and cook for 5 minutes. Drain, discarding the liquid. Put the jelly in a small china bowl set over a saucepan of simmering water and stir the jelly until it has melted. If there are still lumps, put it through a strainer and return it to the clean bowl over simmering water. Squeeze the oranges and the lemon. Stir in the mustard, the port, the orange and lemon juice, the blanched peel and the chopped shallot or onion. Cook for 5 minutes. Meanwhile mix the arrowroot to a paste in a small cup with 1 tablespoon of water. Add to the mixture, stir in and cook for another 2–3 minutes, then pour into a jar and leave to cool before sealing. Keep for at least a week before eating. It will keep for about two months, sealed in a cool place, but should be kept in the refrigerator once opened.

Stuffings/nut and bread

nut stuffing

Use to stuff a 4lb chicken. This is especially delicious when used in a poached chicken, served with boiled rice and a cream sauce made with some of the stock from the poached chicken. Allow an extra 20 minutes for the stuffing when cooking the bird

2 *tablespoons chopped onion*

1 *tablespoon butter*

2 *oz ground veal*

2 *oz ground suet*

2 *tablespoons chopped apple*

2 *tablespoons chopped almonds*

2 *tablespoons chopped pistachio nuts*

pinch of sugar

pinch of mace

pinch of ground coriander

1 *egg*

salt and pepper

Sauté the chopped onion slowly in the butter. Add the veal and cook, stirring often, until evenly browned all over. Remove from the heat and allow to cool. Stir in the ground suet, chopped apple, nuts and seasonings. Beat the egg and stir it in. The stuffing is now ready and can be used immediately.

corn bread stuffing

Use to stuff a medium-size turkey weighing between 10 and 14lb

1 *medium-size onion*

4 *tablespoons (½ stick) butter*

½ *lb pork sausage meat*

1 *turkey liver*

½ *lb corn bread crumbs*

3–4 *tablespoons chopped parsley*

salt and pepper

Chop the onion and sauté it in the butter until a pale golden color. Lift out with a slotted spoon, leaving the fat in the pan, and transfer to a large mixing bowl. Fry the sausage meat in the same pan, breaking it up as it cooks with two wooden spoons. Chop the turkey liver. When the sausage meat is half-cooked, add the liver, stir in and fry all together. Add the meat mixture to the onion and mix well. Add the bread crumbs and parsley and stir until well mixed, adding salt and pepper to taste. Allow to cool completely before using to stuff the turkey.

celery and bread crumb stuffing

Use to stuff a goose or turkey or make half the quantity if you are intending to stuff a capon, duck or large chicken

2 *heads celery*

4 *cups soft white bread crumbs*

½ *teaspoon ground mace*

3 *large eggs*

8 *tablespoons (1 stick) butter, semi-melted*

1 *teaspoon salt*

2 *teaspoons black peppercorns*

Clean and chop, quite finely, the best parts of the celery. Mix with the bread crumbs. Crush the peppercorns roughly in a mortar, and add with the salt and mace. Beat the eggs and stir them in, then the semi-melted butter. Mix the ingredients together and use.

Pasta/sauces

spaghetti with chicken sauce

one 3½ lb chicken

2 onions

3 carrots

3 leeks

3 stalks celery

4 tablespoons (½ stick) butter

3 tablespoons olive oil

2 cloves garlic

one 2 lb can tomatoes

6 oz mushrooms

1½ lb spaghetti

salt and pepper

SERVES 6

Half-cover the chicken with hot water in a heavy pot. Cut 1 onion, 1 carrot, 1 leek and 1 celery stalk in half and put them around the chicken; add a little salt. Bring to the boil, reduce heat, cover and simmer gently for 1 hour. Leave the bird to cool in the stock. Lift it out and strain the stock. Cut the chicken from the bones, discarding the skin, and cut it up in largish pieces. Chop the remaining onion and leeks. Melt 2 tablespoons butter and 3 tablespoons oil in a large frying pan and sauté the chopped onion and leeks in it until slightly colored and softened. Meanwhile chop the remaining carrots and cook them in a little boiling water; then drain. Add the carrots to the onion and leeks, with the chopped celery. Stir around now and then, and after about 5 minutes of gentle cooking add the crushed garlic, then the canned tomatoes, chopped roughly and drained of their juice. Stir around for 3–4 minutes, meanwhile reheating the chicken stock which should be strong and well flavored; if it is not, boil to reduce it. Then pour 1¼ cups of it into the pan. Simmer gently for 20 minutes, adding salt and pepper to taste. Cut the mushrooms in halves or quarters according to size. Melt 2 tablespoons of butter in a small frying pan and sauté the mushrooms until soft. When the sauce is ready, add the chopped chicken and reheat for a few minutes, then add the mushrooms and keep the sauce warm while you cook the spaghetti in plenty of salted boiling water until tender; drain and serve with the chicken and vegetable sauce poured over it.

spaghetti with quick clam sauce

3 tablespoons butter

1 shallot or small onion

1 clove garlic

one 8 oz can minced clams

⅝ cup white wine, or clam juice

⅝ cup heavy whipping cream

2 tablespoons chopped parsley

1 lb spaghetti

salt and pepper

SERVES 4–5

Chop the shallot or onion, crush the garlic, heat the butter and cook the chopped shallot until it is a pale golden color. Add the crushed garlic and cook for a few moments longer. Add the wine or clam juice; open the can of clams and drain the liquid into the pan. Simmer gently for 8 minutes. Stir in the cream, reheat, and add pepper to taste. Add the clams and reheat without allowing it to boil. Add the parsley and keep warm while you cook the spaghetti in plenty of boiling salted water until tender. Drain well and serve with the sauce poured over.

Pasta/sauces and garnishes

spaghetti carbonara

¾ lb bacon slices

1 onion

3 oz Parmesan cheese

6 oz mushrooms

4 tablespoons (½ stick) butter

3 eggs

1¼ cups heavy whipping cream

1½ lb spaghetti

salt and pepper

SERVES 6

Cut the bacon slices in 1-inch strips and chop the onion. Grate the Parmesan cheese and cut the mushrooms in thick slices. Melt 2 tablespoons of butter in a frying pan and sauté the onion until a pale golden color, then add the bacon strips. Fry until the bacon is crisp, remove the grease, then put aside in a warm place. Cook the sliced mushrooms in the remaining 2 tablespoons of butter until softened: add them to the bacon and onion mixture, leaving their juice behind. Keep hot. Beat the eggs – if using extra large eggs leave out one of the whites – and mix the rest thoroughly with the cream. When well blended, stir in the grated Parmesan cheese, some pepper and a little salt. Cook the spaghetti in plenty of boiling salted water until tender; drain and turn into a large hot bowl or casserole and stir in the bacon, onion and mushroom mixture. Pour in the egg, cream and cheese mixture quickly. Lift the spaghetti with two forks to mix well, and serve immediately. All the ingredients must be kept as hot as possible and mixed quickly, otherwise there will not be enough heat to cook the egg yolks.

spaghetti with mussel sauce

Eight large clams can be substituted for the mussels, but they will probably need cooking for 4–5 minutes longer to open the shells

1 quart mussels

⅝ cup white wine

2 tablespoons butter

1 shallot

1 clove garlic

⅝ cup heavy whipping cream

2 tablespoons chopped parsley

1 lb spaghetti or noodles

salt and pepper

SERVES 4

Put the mussels in a deep pan with the wine. Cook over medium heat with the lid on for 4–5 minutes or until the shells have opened. Lift out the mussels with a slotted spoon and boil up the stock until it has reduced slightly. Strain into a measuring pitcher; you should have about 1 cup. Take the mussels out of their shells and keep them warm in a covered bowl. Crush the garlic, chop the shallot finely and melt the butter in a saucepan. Cook the finely chopped shallot until a pale golden color and add the crushed garlic halfway through. Pour on the strained stock, bring to the boil and simmer uncovered for 10 minutes. Add the cream and season with pepper. Chop the mussels and add to the sauce; reheat for a few moments without allowing it to boil, then add the parsley. Keep warm while you cook the spaghetti or noodles in plenty of salted boiling water until tender; drain, cover generously with the sauce and serve as soon as possible.

vegetable sauce for pasta

This can be served as a large vegetable dish in its own right rather than as a sauce, but is good when poured over noodles or other pasta

¼ lb small carrots
¼ lb zucchini squash
¼ lb mushrooms
1 bunch scallions
1 small cauliflower
¼ lb green beans
½ lb tomatoes
6 tablespoons (¾ stick) butter
1 tablespoon flour
1¼ cups chicken stock
⅝ cup cream
pinch of mace or nutmeg
1½ lb noodles or pasta
salt and pepper
SERVES 6

Cut up the carrots, the zucchini and the mushrooms into thick chunks. Clean the scallions and cut off the ends but leave them whole. Divide the cauliflower into sprigs. Cut the beans into 1-inch pieces. Peel the tomatoes and chop them coarsely. Cook the carrots, zucchini, onions, cauliflower and beans separately, one after the other in lightly salted boiling water. Remove them when they are still quite firm and crisp and not overcooked. As soon as each vegetable is cooked, drain well in a colander, then transfer to a large bowl in a warm place. Mix them all together well. Cook the mushrooms in 2 tablespoons of butter in a frying pan, then add them to the bowl of vegetables. Cook the tomatoes briefly in another 2 tablespoons of butter and add to the vegetables. Then make the sauce: melt the remaining butter, add the flour and cook, stirring, for 2–3 minutes. Heat the stock and stir it in. Simmer until smooth, add the cream and season with salt and pepper and a pinch of mace or nutmeg. If necessary, a little of the reserved cooking water can be used to thin the sauce. When it is smooth and well-flavored, mix with the vegetables and keep warm while you cook the noodles or pasta in plenty of boiling salted water until tender; drain and serve with the vegetables poured over.

buckwheat spaghetti with vegetable garnish

1 onion
1 carrot
1 leek
2 tablespoons butter
2 tablespoons olive oil
dash of soy sauce
pinch of sesame salt
½ lb buckwheat spaghetti
salt and pepper
SERVES 2–3

Set a large pan of lightly salted water to come to the boil. Meanwhile cut the onion, the carrot and the leek in half and slice each of them thinly. Heat the butter and the oil in a frying pan and sauté the sliced onion until it is slightly softened. Add the leek, then the carrot. When all are cooked but still crisp, add salt and pepper to taste and the soy sauce. Keep warm while you cook the buckwheat spaghetti in the boiling salted water until tender; drain well. Serve with the vegetables spooned over the buckwheat spaghetti, and sprinkle with sesame salt.

Grains/rice, wheat and couscous

buckwheat kasha with egg

Serve hot with a bowl of cold yogurt

1 egg
½ cup buckwheat
2 tablespoons butter
dash of soy sauce
salt and pepper

SERVES 2

Beat the egg and stir it into the buckwheat until well mixed. Melt the butter in a heavy pan and add the buckwheat mixture. Stir well for 3–4 minutes, until the mixture is coated with fat. Heat 1 cup water until boiling and pour into the pan. Add salt and simmer gently with the lid on for about 15 minutes. Add salt and pepper to taste and the dash of soy sauce.

cracked wheat risotto

This can be served as an accompaniment to broiled meat, or as a dish on its own topped with natural yogurt

½ cup (1 stick) butter
1 onion
½ lb cracked wheat
2 cups chicken stock
salt

SERVES 3–4

Chop the onion, melt the butter in a frying pan and sauté the chopped onion until a pale golden color. Add the cracked wheat and cook gently over low heat for 10 minutes, stirring often. Heat the stock and pour into the pan enough to cover the ingredients generously. Add salt and bring to boiling point; reduce heat, cover the pan and simmer for 10 minutes or until all the stock is absorbed. If this happens before the wheat has softened, add a little water.

cracked wheat salad

¾ cup cracked wheat
5 or 6 scallions
½ lb tomatoes
½ cup chopped parsley
4 tablespoons sunflower seed oil, or other light oil
2 tablespoons lemon juice
salt and pepper

SERVES 3–4

Soak the cracked wheat for about 45 minutes in cold water, then drain and squeeze out as much moisture as possible with your hands. Chop the parsley and the scallions, using the best of the green parts as well as the white. Peel and chop the tomatoes and drain off the juice. Mix all the vegetables with the wheat. Stir in the oil and lemon juice and add salt and pepper to taste.

couscous with vegetables

½ lb couscous
2 lb carrots
6–8 oz frozen peas, preferably petits pois
4 tablespoons (½ stick) butter
salt and pepper

SERVES 4

Pour 1 cup cold water over the couscous and leave for 10 minutes, then pour into a strainer. Slice the carrots and put them in a saucepan with lightly salted boiling water. Place the strainer with the couscous over the pan and cover the strainer. Boil the peas separately in lightly salted water, drain and keep hot. When the carrots are cooked, the couscous should be heated through. If not, lift out the carrots with a slotted spoon and leave the couscous for another 10 minutes over boiling water. When all is cooked, mix together and add the butter cut in small pieces. Add salt and pepper to taste.

rice and yogurt salad

1 *cup long-grain rice*

1 *medium-size onion*

2 *tablespoons oil*

½ *lb tomatoes*

2–3 *oz frozen peas, preferably petits pois*

⅝ *cup yogurt*

2 *tablespoons chopped fresh herbs*

juice of ½ lemon

salt and pepper

SERVES 3–4

Cook the rice in 2 quarts boiling salted water; drain well. Chop the onion and cook in the oil until soft and pale golden in color. Peel the tomatoes and chop them, discarding seeds and juice. Mix the onion and the tomatoes with the rice. Cook the peas and stir them in, then the yogurt and the chopped herbs. Season with salt and pepper and add a little lemon juice. For a hot version, use 2 tablespoons of butter instead of oil to cook the onions, add the chopped tomatoes during the last few minutes of cooking to soften them and leave out the lemon juice.

vegetables with brown rice

2 *tablespoons butter*

2 *tablespoons oil*

1 *medium-size onion*

4 *small carrots*

2 *stalks celery*

¼ *lb mushrooms*

⅞ *cup (6 oz) brown rice*

2 *cups chicken stock*

salt and pepper

SERVES 3–4

Put the stock over medium or low heat. Melt the butter and oil in a frying pan. Chop the onion and sauté it gently until it starts to color. Slice the carrots and cook them gently in lightly salted water for 5 minutes. Drain, and add to the frying pan. Chop the celery and the mushrooms; add. Rinse and drain the rice, and add; stir until all the ingredients are coated with fat and well mixed. Heat the stock and add, with salt and pepper to taste, and cover the pan. Simmer gently for 40–45 minutes, stirring occasionally and adding more stock if needed. At the end of this time the rice should be tender and all the liquid absorbed. If it is not, uncover the pan and cook until the moisture has just disappeared.

polenta

This can be served either as a snack with drinks or as an accompaniment to a mixed grill. It is also good when cut into rounds and topped with a poached or fried egg

¾ *cup corn meal (polenta)*

2 *tablespoons bacon fat or oil*

salt

SERVES 4

Bring 2 cups lightly salted water to the boil and shake in the polenta. Cook gently for about 4 minutes, stirring constantly. When it has become thick and smooth, turn out onto a wet board and shape it with a spatula into a rectangle about ½ inch thick. Leave to cool. Cut into rectangles about 3 inches by 1 inch; fry these on both sides in the bacon fat or oil. Serve immediately.

Desserts/puddings

Christmas pudding

This is usually made well in advance of Christmas but can be eaten straight away

1½ lb seedless raisins
½ lb mixed candied peel
½ lb glacé cherries
¼ lb chopped almonds
¾ lb shredded suet
¾ lb soft white bread crumbs
8 eggs
¼ pint stout or dark beer
6 tablespoons brandy

MAKES 3 PUDDINGS, EACH TO SERVE 6–8

Chop the peel and cut the cherries in half. Mix together with the raisins, almonds, suet and bread crumbs. Beat the eggs well and stir in; add the stout and brandy. Leave for a few hours, or overnight. Butter three pudding bowls well, and spoon the mixture into them. Do not pack it down too tightly; leave at least an inch at the top. Cover each with a buttered piece of aluminum foil and tie over that a square of cloth. Half-fill a very large pan with boiling water and stand the bowls in it not touching each other. The water should come halfway up the sides of the bowls; if necessary put an upside-down pie plate under them, or something similar. Cover the pan and bring back to the boil; boil steadily for 6 hours, adding more boiling water as needed to keep the level halfway up the sides of the bowls. When done, lift out the bowls and leave them to cool. Wrap each pudding in a clean cloth and store in a cool place until Christmas. On Christmas Day, steam them again for 4–6 hours; turn out on a flat dish to serve, and stick a sprig of holly in the top. Warm 3 tablespoons of brandy in a ladle and set a match to it; pour immediately over the pudding and carry it to the table flaming. Serve with brandy or rum butter or hard sauce.

castle puddings

3 eggs
6 tablespoons sugar
¾ cup flour
1 teaspoon grated lemon peel
6 tablespoons (¾ stick) butter, semi-melted
¾ cup golden syrup, or light maple syrup
juice of ½ lemon

SERVES 4

Preheat the oven to 350°F. Beat the eggs until very light and almost frothy, adding the sugar by degrees and beating continuously. Then shake in the flour, a little at a time, and beat in, and lastly stir in the semi-melted butter. Alternatively, all this may be speedily done in a food processor. When all is well mixed, pour into small buttered molds, shaped like tiny buckets. Stand them on a baking sheet and bake for 20 minutes. Turn the puddings out of their molds to serve, and accompany with a sauce made by combining the syrup and lemon juice, and heating the mixture gently. Traditionally, they are also accompanied by a small pitcher of cream.

queen of puddings

1¼ cups milk
2 strips lemon peel
2 tablespoons butter
½ cup sugar
4 tablespoons soft white bread crumbs
3 eggs
3 tablespoons raspberry jam

SERVES 4–5

Put the milk into a pan with the lemon peel and bring slowly to the boil. Remove from the heat, cover the pan and leave for 10 minutes. Discard the lemon peel, add the butter and 2 tablespoons of sugar, and return to the heat. Stir until the butter has melted and the sugar dissolved. Remove from the heat and stir in the bread crumbs. Leave to cool for another 10 minutes. Preheat the oven to 325°F. Separate the eggs, reserving whites. Lightly beat the egg yolks, and stir into the mixture; pour into a well-buttered ovenproof dish and bake for 30 minutes. Take from the oven and leave to cool slightly; turn the oven down to 250°F. Warm the jam and spread it over the pudding. Beat the egg whites until stiff, and fold in the remaining sugar to make a meringue mixture. Spoon this over the jam, covering the pudding completely. Return to the cooler oven and bake for 30 minutes, or until the top of the meringue is firm and lightly colored. This pudding can be served immediately, or kept warm for some time without spoiling. It is also good cold and is usually served with cream.

seven cup pudding

¾ cup soft white bread crumbs

¾ cup dried sultanas (or raisins)

¾ cup currants

¾ cup sugar

¾ cup flour

2 oz chopped orange and lemon peel

2 oz almonds, coarsely chopped

2 teaspoons ground ginger

1 teaspoon ground cinnamon

1 teaspoon mixed spice

pinch of salt

1 egg

⅝ cup milk

1 teaspoon baking soda

1 teaspoon wine vinegar

SERVES 6–8

Mix all the ingredients except the egg, milk, baking soda and vinegar. Break the egg into a teacup and cover with the milk. Stir into the pudding mixture. Dissolve the soda in the vinegar for a minute or two, then stir into the mixture. Stir all together well, then turn into a clean well-buttered heatproof bowl; place in boiling water in a large pan, and steam for 4–6 hours, with the bowl covered with foil, and the pan with the lid on. The boiling water should come halfway up the sides of the bowl; replenish the water as needed as the level drops. Turn out the pudding onto a flat platter and serve with cream or a custard sauce.

bread and butter pudding

3–4 thin slices white bread

2 eggs

2–3 tablespoons butter

2 tablespoons raisins

1¼ cups milk

3 tablespoons vanilla sugar (see recipe, page 126), or plain sugar and ¼ vanilla pod

SERVES 4

If you have no homemade vanilla sugar, heat the milk with the vanilla pod in it; when it reaches boiling point, remove from the heat, cover the pan and let stand for 20 minutes. Keeping the crusts on, butter the bread and cut each slice in four triangles. Lay them in layers in a buttered ovenproof dish, and scatter the raisins over each layer. If using homemade vanilla sugar, put the milk and sugar together in a small pan until the sugar has dissolved. If using a vanilla pod, discard it, add the sugar to the milk, and reheat until the sugar has dissolved. Preheat the oven to 325°F. Beat the eggs, and gradually add the milk and sugar mixture, beating in. Pour the resulting mixture through a sieve into the side of the dish so that the top layer of bread is not submerged. Bake for 1 hour until set and a light golden brown. Serve immediately.

Eve's pudding

A most delicious variation of this can also be made by adding fresh or frozen blackberries (about ½ lb) to the apples when cooking them, but the traditional version of the pudding is this one

1 lb cooking apples
9 tablespoons sugar
6 tablespoons (¾ stick) butter
½ cup self-rising flour
2 eggs

SERVES 5

Peel and slice the apples and put in a saucepan with just enough water to cover the bottom; add 3 tablespoons sugar and cook gently over medium heat until soft. Turn into a buttered soufflé dish. Preheat oven to 350°F. Cream the butter and the rest of the sugar together thoroughly. Beat the eggs and sift the flour. Add them, alternately, to the creamed butter, a little at a time, beating constantly. Spoon over the apples, being careful to cover them completely. Bake for 30 minutes or until golden brown and puffy. Serve this pudding as soon as possible after baking, with cream.

rice pudding

¼ cup (2 oz) short-grain rice
2 tablespoons sugar
2½ cups milk
3 tablespoons butter

SERVES 3–4

Preheat the oven to 300°F. Wash the rice, drain, and put it into a buttered pie plate. Add the sugar and pour the milk over the rice and sugar. Mix with a fork, then dot with butter. Bake for 2 hours, or until the top is nicely browned and almost all the milk has been absorbed by the rice. Serve hot or cold.

cheesecake

¾ cup graham cracker crumbs
7 tablespoons (⅞ stick) butter
1¼ tablespoons light brown sugar
1 cup sugar
2 egg yolks
⅝ cup heavy whipping cream
two 8-oz packages cream cheese
1 tablespoon lemon juice, or grated peel of
½ orange

SERVES 6

Preheat oven to 350°F. Melt 3 tablespoons butter. Reserving a spoonful of the graham cracker crumbs, mix the rest with the butter and the brown sugar until well blended. With two-thirds of this mixture line the bottom and sides of a round baking pan. Bake for 8 minutes. Cool. If you have a food processor, the ingredients for the filling can be put in all together. Otherwise, cream the remaining butter and sift in the white sugar. Beat in the egg yolks and the whipping cream. Beat the cream cheese in a separate bowl until free of lumps and then beat the first mixture into the cheese. Stir in the lemon juice or the grated orange peel, whichever is preferred as a flavoring. When all is smooth and well mixed, pour into the crust in the baking pan, and scatter the reserved graham cracker crumbs over the top. Chill in the refrigerator for several hours before serving.

pumpkin pie

one 2-lb pumpkin
¾ lb short pastry (see recipe, page 126)
2 eggs
¾ cup brown sugar
½ teaspoon salt
1 teaspoon ground cinnamon
½ teaspoon ground nutmeg

¼ teaspoon ground cloves
1½ cups evaporated milk
¼ oz fresh ginger or ½ teaspoon ground ginger

SERVES 6

Preheat the oven to 350°F. Cut the pumpkin in half, scrape out the seeds, and place the two halves in ½ inch of water in a baking pan and bake for about 1 hour, or until the flesh is soft when pierced with a cooking fork. Scoop out the flesh and press it through a medium-mesh sieve. Drain thoroughly. Roll out the pastry and line a pie pan. Bake the pastry for 10 minutes, then cool. Reset the oven to 450°F. Beat the eggs thoroughly, stir in the drained pumpkin puree and the sugar, salt, spices and evaporated milk. Peel the ginger and chop it finely, if not using ground ginger. Stir the ginger into the pumpkin mixture and pour into the pastry shell. Bake the pie for 15 minutes, then turn off heat; leave the pie in the oven. Remove after 45 minutes, and refrigerate to chill before serving.

buttered apples

1½ lb cooking apples
6–8 tablespoons (¾–1 stick) butter
3–4 tablespoons sugar
5–6 slices dry white bread
¾ cup heavy whipping cream

SERVES 5–6

Peel the apples and slice them thickly. Melt 2 tablespoons butter in a frying pan and cook as many of the sliced apples as will fit comfortably in one layer. Sprinkle over them 1 tablespoon of the sugar and sauté the apples gently, turning them now and then, until soft. Lift them out with a slotted spoon and keep them warm while you cook a second batch, adding more butter and sugar. While the apples are cooking, remove the crusts from the bread, and cut each slice in a round, allowing one per person. When all the apples are done, and removed from the pan, add more butter to the pan and fry the rounds of bread. Turn them often until they are golden on both sides. Lay them in a shallow, flat-bottomed bowl and spoon the sliced apples carefully onto them, making a mound on each one. Pour any remaining juice over the apples. Whip the cream and top each with a dollop of whipped cream. Serve as soon as possible. If preparing slightly in advance, do not add the cream until just before serving.

dried-fruit salad

½ lb mixed dried fruit: apples, pears, apricots, peaches, prunes, figs
2 tablespoons raisins
½ teaspoon grated orange peel
½ teaspoon grated lemon peel
2 tablespoons sugar
juice of 1 orange
2 tablespoons coarsely chopped almonds

SERVES 4–5

Cover the fruit with cold water, bring to the boil and cook fairly quickly until soft but not disintegrated. (The timing varies widely according to the fruit; already-soft fruit of good quality should take about 15 minutes.) If there is more than about ½ cup of liquid in the pan, take out the fruit and boil the liquid down to that amount. At the end of the cooking time add the raisins, the grated peel and the sugar. Leave to cool, then stir in the orange juice and the chopped nuts. Serve while still warm, or after cooling, but do not chill. Serve with whipped cream or a mixture of lightly whipped cream and yogurt.

Desserts/fruits, fools and mousses

a tropical fruit salad

2 *guavas*
4 *kiwi fruit (Chinese gooseberries)*
8 *lychees*
2 *passion fruit*
juice of 2 limes
sugar to taste
SERVES 4

Peel the guavas and cut them in small cubes.
Peel the kiwi fruit, cut them in half and then
in quite thick slices. Peel the lychees, cut
them in half and remove the seeds. Mix all
the fruits together in a bowl. Cut the passion
fruit in half and scrape the pulp from the skin;
spoon over the other fruits. Mix the lime juice
with the fruits, adding some sugar if
necessary. Serve in glass bowls.

green and yellow fruit salad

1 *small honeydew melon*
½ *large pineapple*
4 *kiwi fruit (Chinese gooseberries)*
juice of 2 limes
SERVES 4

Cut the melon in half, scoop out the seeds,
and peel off the outer rind. Cut the flesh in
cubes, and put into a glass bowl. Slice the
pineapple thickly, remove the center and the
outer rind from each slice and cut in chunks.
Peel the kiwi fruit, and cut in slices; add to
the bowl. Pour in the lime juice and mix all
together lightly. Chill well before serving.

apricots in white wine

These are delicious eaten at the end of a
meal, with coffee. They are usually passed
around in their jar, and a narrow fork is useful
for fishing them out

Get the best dried apricots you can find and
wash them carefully. Pack loosely into jars
and cover with any fairly sweet, but good,
white wine such as Sauternes. Screw the lids
on tightly and leave for a week before eating.

mango fool

1 *large ripe mango*
2 *tablespoons lime juice*
1¼ *cups yogurt*
SERVES 3–4

Peel the mango and cut the flesh from the
seed. Put it into a blender or food processor
with the lime juice and the yogurt. Blend
until smooth, then pour into 3–4 small glasses
and chill for a couple of hours before serving.

prune mousse

½ *lb dried prunes*
2 *cups cold tea*
4 *tablespoons sugar*
2 *tablespoons brandy or* 1 *tablespoon lemon juice*
1¼ *cups heavy whipping cream*
3 *egg whites*
SERVES 4–5

Soak the prunes overnight in the cold tea;
then add the sugar and cook slowly until soft.
Lift them out with a slotted spoon and discard
the seeds. Put the prunes in a blender with
enough of the liquid from the pan to make a
thick puree. Add the brandy or lemon juice to
sharpen the flavor. Whip the cream until stiff
but not dry, and fold in. Beat the egg whites
stiffly and fold in. Chill in the refrigerator.

coffee mousse

¾ cup freshly made double-strength black coffee

four 1-oz squares good dark unsweetened chocolate

½ cup sugar

3 envelopes (¾ oz) powdered gelatine

3 egg yolks

generous ¾ cup milk

1¼ cups heavy whipping cream

SERVES 6

Melt the chocolate in half the coffee, over gentle heat, adding half of the sugar and stirring in. Dissolve the gelatine in the remaining coffee, then mix all together. Beat the egg yolks in a mixing bowl with the remaining sugar. Bring the milk to boiling point and pour into the egg mixture; stir. Set the bowl over a pan of very hot but not boiling water, and stir until the mixture is slightly thickened. Pour this into the chocolate mixture and stir together. Cool in a sink half-full of cold water, stirring now and then. When quite cold, whip the cream and fold it in. Pour into a soufflé dish and chill until set.

petits pots de crème au café

This is very rich and one wants only a very small amount. It can also be made with light cream, or half-and-half, but the smoothness of the heavy whipping cream is delicious

4 tablespoons freshly made double-strength black coffee

1¼ cups heavy whipping cream

2 egg yolks

1½ tablespoons sugar

SERVES 4

Preheat the oven to 300°F. Heat the coffee and the cream together. Beat the egg yolks with the sugar. When the coffee mixture is almost boiling, pour it into the egg yolk mixture. Mix well, then pour through a strainer into tiny ovenproof dishes. Fill a baking pan half-full of hot water and set the dishes in carefully. Bake for about 25 minutes or until they are just set.

sauce à la vanille

This delicious sauce goes well with most puddings, stewed fruit, baked apples or any kind of ice cream

½ vanilla pod

1¼ cups milk

2 egg yolks

2 tablespoons sugar

SERVES 4

Put the vanilla pod into the milk and heat slowly to boiling point. Remove from the heat, cover the pan and leave to infuse for 20 minutes. Put the egg yolks into a bowl and beat with an electric beater or whisk for about 2 minutes, adding the sugar by degrees. When blended into a thick and creamy paste, reheat the milk almost to boiling point; remove the pod and pour the milk in, continuing to whisk as you do so. Set the bowl over a saucepan of boiling water over heat and stir with a wooden spoon until slightly thickened—it will thicken more on cooling. If the sauce is to be served hot, allow it to cool slightly as it should not be scalding hot. It can then be kept warm over hot (not boiling) water. If it is to be served cold, stand it in a sink half-full of cold water to cool as quickly as possible; stir it as often as possible so as to prevent a skin forming.

wheat germ ice cream

2 eggs + 2 yolks

generous ¼ cup vanilla sugar (see recipe, page 126), or plain sugar and ½ vanilla pod

1¼ cups milk

1¼ cups heavy whipping cream

2 oz sweetened wheat germ

SERVES 6

If you have no homemade vanilla sugar, put half a vanilla pod in the milk, heat to boiling, cover, remove from heat, and leave it for 20 minutes before starting to make the ice cream. Beat the eggs and the egg yolks together in a heatproof mixing bowl with an electric beater. Add the vanilla sugar (or plain sugar if you have none) and continue to beat. Heat the milk (after discarding the vanilla pod, if used) until just about to boil; add to the eggs, continuing to beat until incorporated. Place the bowl over a pan of boiling water over medium heat, and stir until it thickens slightly. Pour through a strainer into a clean bowl and set the bowl in a sink full of cold water. Stir it now and then as it cools, to prevent a skin forming. When the mixture has cooled, beat the cream until semi-whipped, and fold it in. Pour into an ice cream maker and freeze until semi-frozen. Then stir in the wheat germ and continue freezing until set. Alternatively, if you do not have an ice cream maker, freeze the mixture in freezer trays, covered with aluminum foil. After an hour, beat the mixture with a fork and add the wheat germ before returning it to the freezer.

coffee granita

2½ cups freshly made strong coffee

generous ½ cup sugar

SERVES 4–5

Put the sugar into a heavy saucepan with ⅝ cup of water and bring to the boil. Boil gently for 5 minutes, stirring until the sugar has dissolved. Cool both the freshly made coffee and the syrup for a few minutes by standing in a sink half-full of cold water. Then stir the two together, mix well, pour into an ice cream maker and freeze until set. Alternatively, if you do not have an ice cream maker, freeze the mixture in freezer trays, covered with foil. The mixture should be stirred every half-hour with a fork until set but still quite soft. Serve in wine glasses.

hazelnut ice cream

This can also be made with blanched almonds instead of hazelnuts

2 oz hazelnuts, blanched

2 tablespoons sugar

2 eggs + 2 yolks

⅜ cup (2 oz) vanilla sugar (see recipe, page 126), or plain sugar and ½ vanilla pod

1¼ cups milk

1¼ cups heavy whipping cream

SERVES 6

If you have no vanilla sugar, put half a vanilla pod into the milk, and heat to boiling point. Cover the pan, remove from the heat, and let stand for 20 minutes. Put the hazelnuts into a heavy frying pan, scatter the sugar over them and cook, stirring constantly, over a fairly high heat, until the sugar caramelizes (the nuts will turn a golden brown and the whole pan will smoke slightly). Turn onto an oiled surface—marble or glass is best; when cool, break in pieces and chop, in a food processor preferably, until reduced to a medium-fine consistency; an uneven texture does not matter, it even improves the ice cream. Beat the eggs and the yolks with the vanilla sugar, or plain sugar in a heatproof bowl until thick. Remove the vanilla pod from the milk, if necessary, and heat the milk until almost boiling. Pour into the egg mixture, beating constantly. Set the bowl over a pan of simmering water and stir constantly until slightly thickened, about 8 minutes. Strain into a clean bowl and stand in a sink of ice-cold water, stirring now and then to prevent a skin forming. When cool, whip the cream until semi-thick, and when the egg custard is cool, fold in the cream. Pour into an ice cream maker, and freeze. When almost frozen, fold in the crushed nut mixture and continue to freeze until set. If you have no ice cream maker freeze the mixture in freezer trays, covered with aluminum foil. After about 1 hour, beat the mixture with a fork, fold in the crushed nuts, and continue to freeze until set.

passion fruit sorbet

12 *passion fruit*
juice of 4 large oranges
juice of 2 limes
½ *cup sugar*
2 *egg whites*
SERVES 4

Cut the passion fruit in half and scoop out the pulp with a teaspoon. Press it through a medium-mesh sieve to remove the seeds. Add the orange and lime juice to the passion fruit. Heat the sugar with ½ cup water in a heavy pan until melted, then boil until reduced to about ½ cup thin syrup. Cool slightly and mix with the fruit juices. Pour into an ice cream maker and freeze until mushy, about 1 hour. Whip the egg whites fairly stiffly and fold into the semi-frozen sorbet. Turn back into the ice cream maker and continue to freeze until set. Alternatively, if you do not have an ice cream maker, freeze the mixture in freezer trays, covered with aluminum foil. When the mixture is still mushy, remove from the freezer and beat with a fork before folding in the egg whites; then continue to freeze.

pineapple sorbet

1 *large pineapple*
½ *cup sugar*
juice of 4 medium-size oranges
1 *tablespoon lime juice or 2 teaspoons lemon juice*
2 *egg whites*
SERVES 5–6

Cut the top and bottom off the pineapple and slice it thickly. Remove the central core from each slice and cut off the outer skin. Cut the slices in cubes and puree them in a food processor or blender. Press the puree through a nylon sieve. You should have about 1¼ cups. Heat the sugar with ½ cup water in a heavy pan. Bring to the boil, reduce heat, and simmer until the sugar dissolves and the mixture reduces to about ½ cup thin syrup. Cool. Squeeze the juice of the oranges. Mix the orange juice with the pineapple juice and the cooled sugar syrup, and add the lime (or lemon) juice; mix well. Pour into an ice cream maker and freeze for about 1 hour, or until mushy. Spoon into a bowl. Stiffly beat the egg whites, and fold into the mixture: continue to freeze. If you do not have an ice cream maker, freeze the mixture in freezer trays, covered with aluminum foil, adding the egg whites as above, when the mixture is semi-frozen. Return to the freezer to set.

Finnish rye bread

2 cakes fresh yeast

3 teaspoons light brown sugar

1 tablespoon melted butter

1½ teaspoons salt

2 cups sifted all-purpose flour

¾ cup rye flour

Put the yeast in a cup with one teaspoon of the brown sugar. Add 4 tablespoons of tepid water. Leave in a warm place for 10 minutes, then stir. Pour into a large warm bowl, add 1 cup tepid water, the melted butter and the salt. Sprinkle in the white flour gradually, then the rye flour. Knead for 4–5 minutes or until smooth, then sprinkle with white flour and leave to rise in a warm place in a covered bowl for 1 hour, by which time it should have doubled in size. Butter a baking sheet and sprinkle with white flour. Knead the dough again for 4–5 minutes and pat into a flat round shape, large enough to fit nicely on the sheet. Leave to rise again for 20 minutes. Preheat the oven to 375°F. Sprinkle with rye flour and bake for 1 hour, watching to make sure it does not become too brown. If this starts to happen, cover with a sheet of aluminum foil. Cool on a wire rack; serve as soon as possible as it is delicious when still very fresh.

corn meal bread

2½ oz corn meal

2 cakes fresh yeast

2 teaspoons sugar

1 cup milk

2 teaspoons salt

4 tablespoons brown sugar

1¾ lb all-purpose flour

Measure 1 cup water into a small pan and bring to the boil. Shake in the corn meal gradually, stirring all the time. Boil gently, continuing to stir for 3–4 minutes or until thick and smooth. Pour into a large mixing bowl and leave to cool. Put the yeast in a cup with 2 teaspoons of sugar and ½ cup tepid water. Leave in a warm place for 10 minutes to prove. Heat the milk briefly, until lukewarm. When the yeast is bubbly, stir it into the cool corn meal. Mix as smoothly as possible, then add the milk, the salt and the brown sugar; mix, then start adding the flour, a cupful at a time. Beat in each addition well with a wooden spoon. Stop adding the flour when the dough clings together nicely and start to knead on a floured board, adding as much of the remaining flour as is needed to give a smooth elastic dough. After at least 6–8 minutes, leave it and wash and dry the mixing bowl and rub it well with butter. Put the dough in the bowl, and turn it over so it gets a light coating of butter all over. Cover loosely with plastic wrap or a cloth, and leave in a warm place for about an hour, until double in size. Punch the dough down, knead again briefly, and divide in two. Preheat the oven to 425°F. Form the dough into loaf shapes; put in two buttered loaf pans and leave to rise again for 30 minutes or so, until again doubled. Bake for 10 minutes, then turn the oven to 350°F and bake for 20 minutes more. Tap the bottoms of the loaves to see if they are done—they should sound hollow. If not, tip them out of the pans and lay them on the oven rack on their sides for another 5 minutes. When done, cool on a wire rack.

white loaf

2 cups sifted all-purpose flour
1 cake fresh yeast
1 teaspoon salt

Put the flour in a large bowl and set in a warm place. Crumble the yeast into a cup and add 2 tablespoons of warm water. Put in a warm place for 10 minutes. Measure 1¼ cups water and heat; dissolve the salt in it. When the yeast mixture has started to become bubbly, make a hole in the center of the flour and pour the mixture in. Add the warm salted water, stirring with a wooden spoon. When it begins to hold together, turn out onto a floured surface and start to knead, sprinkling with flour until it no longer sticks to the working surface. Continue to knead for about 5 minutes in all. By this time it should be smooth and elastic and no longer sticky. Wash out the bowl and dry it. Put back the dough, sprinkle with flour and cover with a cloth. Leave to rise for 2 hours in a warm place. By that time the dough should have doubled in size. Punch it down with your fist and turn out with a rubber spatula. Knead for another 5 minutes, then form it into a loaf shape and put it into a greased tin sprinkled with flour. It should fill it by about half, perhaps slightly more, but by not more than two-thirds. Leave it to rise again for another half hour. After 25 minutes, preheat the oven to 425°F. After 5 minutes more, sprinkle the top of the loaf with flour or brush it with beaten egg yolk, for a shiny crust, and bake in the center of the oven for 45 minutes. Test by turning it out of the pan and knocking it on the bottom—it should have a hollow sound; otherwise put it back in the oven for another 5–10 minutes.

potato bread

This is excellent when toasted or when served with cheese or simply with butter. It keeps well, and when slightly stale can be used to make a delicious stuffing for poultry or fish

1 cake fresh yeast
½ cup sugar
1 cup milk
¾ cup (1½ sticks) butter
2 eggs
¾ cup freshly cooked mashed potato
7 cups sifted white flour
1 tablespoon salt

Put the yeast and 1 tablespoon sugar in a large bowl with ½ cup tepid water; set in a warm place. After 5 minutes, cut the butter in pieces and warm it with the milk. When lukewarm and semi-melted, pour into the bowl with the yeast mixture. Add the remaining sugar and the salt. Beat and add the eggs. Stir well until mixed, then combine with the freshly mashed potato and beat together. When smooth, start adding the flour, one cupful at a time. Beat it in with a wooden spoon, stopping as soon as the dough clings together. Knead for 10 minutes, adding flour if necessary to give a smooth springy dough. Clean the bowl, rub it with butter, and put in the dough. Cover tightly with plastic wrap, and leave in a warm place to rise for 2 hours. Punch down, turn out, and knead again for 5 minutes. Divide it in two, shape it into loaves and turn into buttered loaf pans. Allow to rise again for 1 hour. Meanwhile preheat the oven to 375°F. Bake for at least 45 minutes. Tap the bottom of the loaf to test whether it is fully cooked; it should sound hollow. Stand on a wire rack to cool completely before eating.

Breads/sweet and seasoned

onion bread

This bread is delicious served with pâté

4 cups sifted all-purpose flour

1 cake fresh yeast

1 lb onions

4 tablespoons (½ stick) butter

2 egg yolks

salt and pepper

Warm a large bowl and put the flour in with the salt. Put the yeast in a cup with 3 tablespoons tepid water and stand in a warm place for 10 minutes. Make a well in the center of the flour and pour in the yeast mixture, which should be bubbly. Add 1⅛ cup of water and mix with a wooden spoon. As soon as it holds together, turn the dough out onto a floured surface and knead briskly, sprinkling with more flour as necessary, for 5 minutes. Return to the bowl, cover with a cloth and stand in a warm place for 2 hours. Punch the dough down, turn it out, and knead again for another 5 minutes. Pat into a flat round shape and lay on a greased baking sheet sprinkled with flour. Leave to rise again for 45 minutes while you prepare the onions. Slice them quite finely and cook gently in the butter in a covered pan until soft and a pale golden color. Add salt and pepper, and pile the onions on top of the bread when it is ready to go in the oven. Preheat the oven to 450°F, beat the egg yolks and brush lightly over the onions. Bake for 15 minutes, then turn the oven down to 425°F and bake for a further 30 minutes. Watch to see that the onions do not burn; if they start to become too brown, cover them lightly with aluminum foil.

saffron bread

This beautiful golden yellow bread is delicious when served with hot or cold mixed vegetable dishes

4 cups sifted all-purpose flour

1½ teaspoons salt

1 cake fresh yeast

⅝ cup milk

2 generous pinches of saffron

2 eggs

1 egg yolk (optional)

Put the flour in a warm bowl with the salt. Crumble the yeast in a cup with 4 tablespoons tepid water and leave in a warm place for 10 minutes. Put the milk in a saucepan, add the saffron and bring to boiling point, then leave to cool until lukewarm. Beat the eggs. Make a well in the flour, pour in the yeast mixture, cover with flour, then add the saffron milk and the beaten eggs. Mix well with a wooden spoon, adding a little extra milk or water if needed. Turn out on a floured surface and knead for about 5 minutes. Return to the bowl, cover with a cloth and leave for 1 hour to rise. Punch the dough down with your fist, turn out and knead again for 4–5 minutes. Turn into a buttered loaf pan and leave to rise again for 45 minutes. Preheat the oven to 375°F. You can brush the pastry with a beaten egg yolk for a shiny crust, but this is purely optional. Bake for 30 minutes.

spiced fruit bread

7 cups all-purpose flour

1 teaspoon salt

2 cakes fresh yeast or 2 packages dried yeast

6 tablespoons lard

2 eggs

¾ cup milk

1 cup raisins

½ *cup dried currants*

½ *cup sultanas*

2 *oz cut mixed peel*

¾ *cup sugar*

1 *teaspoon allspice*

1 *tablespoon dark molasses*

Warm a large bowl, put the flour in it with the salt and put the bowl in a warm place. Put the yeast in a cup with 2 tablespoons of tepid water and leave for 10 minutes. Cut the lard in small pieces and rub it into the flour. Beat the eggs in a mixing bowl and pour into a measuring container. Add enough milk and water in equal quantities to make 1⅞ cups. Make a well in the middle of the flour and pour in first the yeast mixture, then the egg mixture. Mix briefly and put in a warm place for 30 minutes. In the meantime, measure the dried fruit into another bowl and put this in a warm place also. Warm the molasses in the top of a double boiler. Turn out the flour mixture and knead until smooth, then return to the bowl and stir in the dried fruit, the sugar, the allspice and the warm molasses. Mix thoroughly, then put in a warm place for 2 hours. Divide the mixture in half, and place in two well-buttered loaf pans, or the pans may be lined with buttered greaseproof paper. Put back in a warm place for 20 minutes; meanwhile preheat the oven to 350°F. Bake the loaves for 1¼ hours, then turn out on a wire rack to cool. Wrap the loaves in a dry cloth and store in an airtight container. To serve, cut in fairly thick slices and spread with butter.

pirog

This Russian yeast pastry is light in texture, similar to brioche but less rich. It is traditionally stuffed with a filling of vegetables such as cabbage and onion, or of mushrooms (see recipes overleaf). Hard-boiled eggs are also sometimes added

4 *cups sifted all-purpose flour*

1 *teaspoon salt*

1½ *cakes fresh yeast*

pinch of sugar

½ *cup (1 stick) butter*

1 *egg + 3 yolks*

⅝ *cup tepid milk*

Put the flour with the salt into a large warm bowl. Crumble the yeast in a cup with the sugar and ⅝ cup tepid water. Stand for 10 minutes in a warm place until it starts to bubble. Heat the butter until almost melted, and beat the egg yolks with the milk. Make a well in the middle of the flour, pour in the yeast mixture and cover with the flour. Pour in the egg and milk mixture and mix well. Turn on to a floured surface and pat out into a rectangle. Dot the butter over the dough in small pieces, then roll it up and knead it to mix, but only for a moment or two; then return to the bowl and cover with a cloth. Leave in a warm place to rise for 2 hours, or until doubled in volume. Punch down, turn out and knead again; it should be slightly easier to work now. Continue to knead, sprinkling with extra flour, until smooth. Beat the eggs. Roll out the dough into a large oval shape and spoon the filling over half of it. Fold over the other half, like an omelette, and seal the edges with beaten egg, pinching them together with floured fingers. Preheat the oven to 400°F and return the bread to a warm place to rise for another 20 minutes; then bake for 20 minutes. Serve hot in slices.

mushroom filling for pirog

½ lb mushrooms
4 tablespoons (½ stick) butter
juice of ½ lemon
4 tablespoons chopped parsley
salt and pepper

Slice the mushrooms and sauté them gently in the butter. When almost softened, add the lemon juice, parsley, and plenty of salt and freshly ground black pepper. Allow to cool before using.

cabbage and onion filling for pirog

1 medium-size onion
3 tablespoons butter
1 head green cabbage
salt and pepper

Melt the butter in a frying pan. Chop the onion and sauté it in the butter. Remove and discard the outer leaves of the cabbage; cut into quarters. Cook the cabbage briskly in boiling salted water until just tender. Drain well and chop, squeezing out all the moisture as soon as it is cool enough to handle. Put in a bowl; add the onions from the frying pan and mix well, seasoning with plenty of salt and black pepper. Cool before filling the pirog.

potato and apple cake

This is an Irish teatime dish and is surprisingly good

1 lb older Idaho potatoes
2 tablespoons butter
1 teaspoon sugar
pinch of salt
1 cup sifted flour
2 cups apple puree

Boil the potatoes until tender; drain. Mash them while they are still hot and beat in the butter. Add a level teaspoon of sugar and a pinch of salt. Shake in the sifted flour bit by bit and beat with a wooden spoon until smooth. Knead lightly and divide it in half. Butter a small cake tin with a removable bottom and roll out each half of the dough on a floured surface to fit. Preheat the oven to 350°F. Lay one circle in the tin and cover with a layer of apple puree. Cover with the second circle of dough and bake for 50 minutes. Sprinkle with sugar and serve hot with cream.

spiced cookies

2½ cups flour
9 oz (2 sticks + 2 tablespoons) butter, at room temperature
2 medium-size eggs, or 1 large egg + 1 yolk
¾ cup light brown sugar
2 teaspoons ground cinnamon
½ teaspoon ground ginger
½ teaspoon ground nutmeg
½ teaspoon ground cloves

Sift the flour and the sugar, separately. Put the flour into a large bowl. Cut the butter into small pieces and rub into the flour. Beat the eggs and add the sugar and the ground spices, beating each in gradually until smooth; combine with the flour and butter. Stir well with a wooden spoon until smooth. The dough will be soft and must be chilled before rolling out. Enclose in plastic wrap and refrigerate overnight. If it is still too soft, put it in the freezer for 20 minutes. Roll out carefully until about ¼ inch thick and cut into shapes. Preheat the oven to 350°F. Lift the shapes with a spatula onto a buttered baking sheet. Bake for 8–10 minutes; allow to cool before lifting the cookies off the baking sheet.

Drinks

sloe gin

This is delicious served as an aperitif

2 *bottles dry gin*

5 *cups sloes*

¾ *lb lump sugar*

Get a gallon-size earthenware crock or jar. Prick each sloe with a strong needle stuck in a cork, and drop the pricked sloes into the crock. Add the gin and the sugar and close tightly. Leave for 2½–3 months, turning and shaking the crock from side to side every two or three days. When the time is up, pour the liquid off, discard the sloes, and bottle; seal tightly until you are ready to drink it.

Monaco

This delicious and virtually non-alcoholic drink can be made quickly and easily

1 *bottle or can any good light beer*

1 *bottle or can any sweet lemon soda*

4 *dashes grenadine*

SERVES 4

Put a dash of grenadine in each of 4 tall glasses. Add several ice cubes and fill up with equal parts of beer and lemon soda. Stir lightly and serve immediately.

lemon vodka

Tarragon and chili also make excellent flavorings for vodka

1 *bottle vodka*

1 *lemon, or* 4–5 *small chili peppers, or* 1 *large sprig fresh tarragon*

SERVES 10–15

Find a pretty bottle of the right size, with a well-fitting stopper or cork, preferably in clear glass, or alternatively two smaller bottles to hold a half-bottle each. Cut the zest from the lemon carefully, to get only the yellow part, cutting lengthwise, in thin strips. Put the lemon strips (or alternatively the peppers or the tarragon) in the bottle(s); fill with vodka, and seal tightly. Leave for at least 10 days, preferably in the refrigerator, since this is best when very cold indeed; it can even be kept safely in the freezer, since the high alcohol content keeps it from freezing.

Irish coffee

4 *jiggers Irish whiskey*

2 *cups freshly made strong black coffee*

1 *teaspoon sugar*

4 *tablespoons heavy whipping cream, very cold*

SERVES 2

Warm two glasses and put in each 1 teaspoon sugar and 2 jiggers whiskey, then the hot coffee. Stir gently, then pour the cold cream over the back of a spoon, so that it floats on the top of the coffee. Serve this drink immediately without stirring.

Turkish coffee

2 *heaping teaspoons ground Turkish coffee*

2 *teaspoons sugar*

4–6 *cardamom seeds (optional)*

SERVES 2

Put the coffee and the sugar into a traditional coffee pot with a narrow neck, or use a small saucepan. Add 4 tablespoons cold water and set over a high heat, stirring until well mixed. Bring to the boil and remove from the heat when the froth rises. Stir briefly, return to the heat and allow to boil up a second time, then pour immediately into small cups, allowing the froth to lie on the surface. Serve hot, but allow the grounds to settle before drinking. The cardamom seeds can be added before the second boiling process.

Basic recipes

basic white sauce

1¼ cups milk, or stock of chicken, fish or vegetables
1 thin slice onion
2 cloves
¼ bay leaf
3 tablespoons butter
2 tablespoons flour
pinch of grated nutmeg
salt and pepper

If using milk and no other flavoring is to be added to the white sauce, the milk should be infused before adding: put it into a small pan with the onion, cloves, and bay leaf. Bring slowly to the boil and immediately remove from the heat. Cover the pan and let stand for 20 minutes. Melt the butter slowly in a heavy pan. Remove from the heat and shake in the flour, stirring until amalgamated. Return to the heat and cook for 1 minute, stirring constantly. Remove from the heat again. Strain the heated milk. Pour it (or the stock) gradually into the pan, stirring constantly until blended. Return to the heat and bring to the boil, stirring. Simmer gently for at least 4 minutes, stirring now and then. Add salt and pepper to taste and the grated nutmeg. Grated cheese or cream should be added at this stage; chopped herbs should be added only at the last moment. This sauce can be served immediately or kept warm over a pan of hot water until needed; in this case beat well before serving.

vanilla sugar

3–4 vanilla pods
2¼ cups sugar

Put the sugar into a glass jar and stick a few vanilla pods upright into the sugar. Fill up the jar with the rest of the sugar and close tightly. Leave for at least a week before using, to allow the vanilla flavor to permeate the sugar. Some people cut the pods in half lengthwise, which increases the flavor, but this gives a sticky brown substance to the sugar, which I find unattractive. If required for another use, a pod can be taken out of the sugar, and used to flavor a dish, then carefully washed, well dried, and replaced in the jar. I find this is rarely necessary, however, as I do not often seem to need the flavor of vanilla without the sweetness of the sugar. As it is used up, the sugar can be replenished; the pods will only need replacing after a year or so.

basic short pastry

When a recipe calls for ½ lb pastry, use the quantities given here. When a recipe calls for 6 oz pastry, make this quantity and put aside a quarter of it. Where a recipe calls for ¾ lb pastry, make double the quantity, and put aside a quarter for another use. For a sweet dish, omit the salt and add a pinch of sugar and a squeeze of lemon juice

2 cups sifted flour
pinch of salt
½ cup (1 stick) butter
¼ cup lard

Make sure both the butter and lard are very cold indeed before starting, and have some ice water available. Sift the flour with the salt into a large bowl. Cut the butter and lard in small pieces and rub them into the flour very quickly; then add just enough ice water to make a soft dough, mixing with the blade of a knife. Handling it as little as possible, form it in a ball, enclose in plastic wrap, and refrigerate for 30 minutes before using.

Index